Irish Regional Policy

Issues in Public Administration is a series of publications dealing with themes and debates in the public sector domain in Ireland.

The series editor is Dr Michael Mulreany, Assistant Director General, Whitaker School of Government and Management at the Institute of Public Administration.

Also in this series:

Protection or Free Trade – The Final Battle
T. K. Whitaker
Dublin: Institute of Public Administration, 2006

An Investigation of the Measurement of Poverty in Ireland
Colin Menton
Dublin: Institute of Public Administration, 2007

Advisers or Advocates? The Impact of State Agencies on Social Policy
Orlaigh Quinn
Dublin: Institute of Public Administration, 2008

Dynamics of Regulation in Ireland: Advocacy, Power and Institutional Interests
Pat Nolan
Dublin: Institute of Public Administration, 2008

Competing in an Uncertain World: Institutional Change in the Irish State
Eddie Lewis
Dublin: Institute of Public Administration, 2010

IRISH REGIONAL POLICY
In Search of Coherence

Kieran Moylan

IPA
INSTITUTE OF PUBLIC
ADMINISTRATION

First published 2011
by the Institute of Public Administration
57–61 Lansdowne Road
Dublin 4
Ireland

ISBN: 978-1-904541-94-3

British Library Cataloguing in Publication Data
A catalogue record for this book is available from the British Library.

Cover design by Alice Campbell, Dublin
Typeset by Carole Lynch, Sligo
Printed in Ireland by Turner Print Group, Longford

Contents

Acknowledgements

This publication stems from research carried out as part of a Doctorate in Governance. I wish to acknowledge the support and assistance of the many people who made this study possible. I am grateful to my Supervisor, Professor Frank Gaffikin, Queen's University Belfast, whose guidance was particularly important in helping me to develop and scope my research proposal and to structure the dissertation.

Sincere thanks are due to the 24 interviewees who participated in the study and offered valuable and distinctive perspectives on current regional policy in Ireland. I am grateful for their insights and for the level of access, openness and co-operation that I received throughout.

The examiners at the viva and in their written reports following the viva provided encouragement and advice on final editing and redrafting, for which I am very grateful.

I would like to acknowledge the support of the Border, Midland and Western Regional Assembly and in particular Mr Gerry Finn, Director, who facilitated my research and Adrian O'Donoghue for proofreading the final draft. My gratitude is due to Richard Boyle and Hannah Ryan in the Publishing Division, IPA and to Brendan O'Brien for preparing the proofs for publication. I also thank the Local Government Management Services Board for their financial support with regard to the course fees over the four years of the DGov programme.

Finally, I would like to thank Mary for her support and patience over many years and also Bridget and Feargal who provided the ongoing encouragement that enabled me to complete this study.

This book is dedicated to the memory of my father, Patrick Moylan (1926–2005).

Preface

The context for regional development is constantly being reshaped by the increasingly globalised economic system which affects regions differently, with the risk that interregional disparities will widen further. The focus of this study is on the coherence of Irish regional policy in this evolving context. It develops and applies a conceptual model of policy coherence and considers the elements of this framework, both internal and external to the state. The study focused on three dimensions of regional policy: investment planning, spatial planning and territorial governance.

The study engages critically with the dominant regional economic growth theories and the influential concepts of territorial cohesion, regional competitiveness and polycentric spatial development. It reviews the literature on typologies of regional policies under the headings of investment-based policies, spatial policies and territorial governance, and examines their relevance to Ireland.

The study combined an analysis of primary and secondary documentary sources and statistical trends with the outcomes of 24 semi-structured interviews conducted between August 2007 and July 2008 with leading personnel in four broad categories: government departments and agencies; subnational public bodies; selected academic experts; and social partner bodies, who are active players in regional policy development, implementation and evaluation processes. The interview transcripts were qualitatively analysed to identify the most significant common themes, and the outcomes are considered in the context of the theoretical literature.

Among the key findings are that regional policy goals are subsidiary to national goals and that Irish regional policy lacks coherence with related policies. The study finds a need for an enhanced role for region-level bodies, which would greatly improve the territorial co-ordination of sectoral policies. It concludes that the policy coherence framework developed for this study is a useful one that could be applied more generally in reviewing public policies.

1

Introduction

There is increasing recognition that regions[1] are the appropriate spatial unit for policy intervention. This reflects a shift to an emphasis on the contribution of regions themselves to managing the impact of the more competitive globalised economic system, rather than a reliance on the directing policies and resources of the state. It implies that coherent regional policies and supportive governance frameworks are required in order to enhance regions' endogenous resources. At the same time, the prevailing paradigms that influence the framing of regional policies are shifting from cohesion to polycentric spatial structuring and competitiveness.

This study focuses on the coherence of Irish regional policy in this evolving context, with an emphasis on three dimensions of regional policy: investment planning processes, spatial planning and territorial governance arrangements. A conceptual model of policy coherence is developed and applied in which the elements of internal and external policy consistency are considered. The study also explores the application of the influential concepts of territorial cohesion, competitiveness and polycentric development to Irish regional policy.

This chapter commences with a brief overview of the principal factors and conceptual frameworks that currently influence the orientation of regional policy. The focus of the study, the overall research aim and specific research objectives are then defined. The following section describes the methodology that was used to gather and interpret the information on which the research findings are based. A summary of the key findings and conclusions and an outline of the structure of this book are then set out. Finally, the utility of the study outcomes to Irish regional policy is considered.

Regional development context

The context for regional development is constantly being reshaped by the more competitive globalised economic system, with increased

1 Throughout this study the term 'region' is meant to imply a subnational administrative area or meso-tier between national government and local government.

internationalisation of investment and a heightened prospect of a widening of existing economic disparities (Pike et al., 2006). Globalisation and trade liberalisation forces affect regions differently and create new competition along regional lines, leading to a self-sustaining concentration of economic activity in core regions, with a concomitant weakening of the competitive position of less attractive regions (Fitzgerald et al., 1999; Organisation for Economic Co-operation and Development (OECD), 2005).

There is a growing recognition of the regional foundations of national competitiveness and that regions are the pivotal sites and the most appropriate spatial units for gaining comparative and collaborative advantage, through the genesis of local milieux of knowledge and innovation, untraded interdependencies and institutional configurations that are most conducive to competitiveness (Gardiner et al., 2004; Rodrígues-Pose and Gill, 2005). As a spatial concept, regions are recognised by the European Union as the most appropriate arena for the coordination of sectoral policies and the most appropriate level for analysis (Commission of the European Communities (CEC), 1999).

At the same time, an evolution is taking place in governance structures, with a hollowing-out of the state and the creation of multiagency configurations and multilevel governance systems (Pike et al., 2006). Diversionary regional policies and the array of (mostly exogenous) instruments previously applied by states to manage spatial economies are less potent than previously. The architects of regional policies must therefore search for new mechanisms to manage the impact of economic change on territories that focus more on regions themselves. Regions are increasingly subject to what Keating (2000: 143) refers to as the 'competitive imperative', and there is a consequent need to design and administer policies at the most appropriate spatial scale, in order to ensure effective delivery of public policy (Adams et al., 2003). Undifferentiated national economic development strategies have tended to treat unequal regions equally, thus widening disparities (Morgan, 2002). Nevertheless, states continue to retain a privileged position controlling, *inter alia*, domestic budgets and institution building (Laffan, 2004).

Within the European Union (EU), the considerable regional disparities that persist both between and within Member States constitute a major challenge to economic integration. Reducing regional disparities has been a priority for the EU for some time and harmonious, balanced and sustainable development is one of the central aims. The Structural and Cohesion Funds account for over one third of the EU budget 2007–2013, while the EU is trying to balance the potentially contradictory aims of global competitiveness and territorial cohesion.

The territorial principle is not well articulated in the Republic of Ireland

and its public administration system operates largely on a functional rather than a territorial basis. The governance structures to support spatial planning and regional development are quite weak (Walsh, 2005). Ireland was relatively unaffected by the wave of regionalisation that swept across Europe from the 1970s, although policies did exist such as the attraction of foreign manufacturers into advanced factory sites in dispersed regional locations. Regional economic disparities were generally narrow during this period.

Interest in regional policy waned with the weakness of the macroeconomic environment in the 1980s, only to re-emerge in response to EU demands for greater regional input into programme planning and monitoring in the 1990s. Economic disparities widened during the 'Celtic Tiger' period and remain wide today. There is a growing consensus that these disparities need to be addressed to minimise their harmful effects on the efficient operation of the national economy (Irish Business and Employers Confederation (IBEC), 2006). The 'regional problem' as it exists today is a double-edged sword, with problems of congestion and pressure on infrastructure and services in the Greater Dublin Area (GDA) and some other cities on one hand and a decline in traditional sectors, inadequate infrastructure and gaps in service provision in many regional locations on the other.

There have been two discernible paradigmatic shifts in the focus of regional policy in recent years. First, there has been a shift from economic and social cohesion as the principal driver of EU regional policy, to a new emphasis on polycentric spatial planning as a means of creating the conditions for balanced sustainable growth within states. Second is the increased focus on competitiveness and employment growth, as expressed in the Lisbon Agenda. There are risks that without countervailing policies to enhance regional growth prospects, the disparities evident in most advanced economies may be exacerbated by the intensified focus on competitiveness (Commins, 2006).

Although these issues are not exclusive to Ireland, this analysis poses serious questions for Ireland, a small open economy that is highly globalised but also highly centralised, with weak regional institutional structures and persistent disparities in regional productivity levels. This evolving socioeconomic, politico-institutional and conceptual context implies that a critical re-examination and reorientation of regional policy approaches and regional governance is now required in Ireland in order to ensure a more coherent policy framework that enables the optimisation of each region's contribution to overall economic and social wellbeing. Furthermore, the decline in Ireland's entitlement to EU receipts means that Irish regional policy is now largely determined domestically, presenting an opportunity to frame and orient regional policy to meet public policy goals that are defined nationally.

Research hypothesis

This study tested the proposition that the coherence of Irish regional policy can be improved. Recognising that many of the issues germane to a study of regional policy in Ireland are multidimensional and contested, the study focused on three dimensions of regional policy: investment planning, spatial planning and territorial governance. It also explored the application of the influential concepts of territorial cohesion, competitiveness and polycentric development to Irish regional policy.

Research aim and objectives

The overall aim of the study was to assess how the coherence of Irish regional policy could be improved, with particular emphasis on investment strategies, spatial planning and the governance of regional policy at central and regional levels, taking account of current influential theoretical perspectives, the politico-institutional setting and the prevailing socio-economic context.

In order to achieve the above aim, the following research objectives were set.

- To review the literature on regional economic growth, the rationale for regional policy and the principal regional policy instruments available, in order to provide a theoretical orientation to the study
- To explore the influential concepts of territorial cohesion, competitiveness and polycentric urban development and how they may apply to Ireland
- To review relevant literature on the concept of policy coherence and to construct a framework within which to assess the coherence of Irish regional policy
- To trace the evolution of Irish regional policy and identify the sources of regional economic disparities in Ireland
- To review regional socioeconomic trends and national and selected sectoral strategies in Ireland
- To elicit the views of leading personnel on the following research questions (themes): the rationale, goals, features, measurement and effectiveness of regional policy in Ireland; the forces that are driving convergence/divergence; the influence of cohesion, polycentric development and competitiveness on the framing of regional policy; strategic investment and spatial planning processes and governance arrangements at central and regional levels

- To summarise and correlate the findings arising from the above analyses
- To draw conclusions on how the coherence of Irish regional policy and the effectiveness of investment planning, spatial planning and regional governance approaches could be improved and to identify the implications of these for Irish regional policy
- To make appropriate recommendations arising from the findings and conclusions.

Methodology

The methodology used combined an analysis of primary and secondary documentary sources and statistical trends with the outcomes of 24 semi-structured interviews with leading personnel in four broad categories: government departments and national agencies, subnational public bodies, selected academic experts and social partner bodies, all of whom are active players in the policy development, implementation and evaluation processes. The use of an exclusively quantitative or qualitative approach was considered insufficient to achieve the aims of the study.

The themes of the semi-structured interviews took account of the research questions, the concepts reviewed in the theoretical literature and the elements of the policy coherence framework developed in this study. A qualitative data analysis approach was used to analyse the interview transcripts and identify the most significant common themes. The findings were correlated with the content analysis of key national and selected sectoral strategies and socioeconomic trends.

Main findings and conclusions

The main findings of the study are that the regional policy debate in Ireland is shifting from a locus of 'regional equity' to one of 'regional efficiency' and the agenda for Irish regional policy is now largely set by the National Spatial Strategy (NSS), with goals that do not easily lend themselves to measurement. Regional policy is viewed as secondary to national policy; it is not significantly influenced by state and non-state policy advocates and its perceived effectiveness has been contingent on the growth of the overall national economy in recent years. The interviewees predicted that the forces of global economic activity are likely to drive further concentration of economic activity, and that the NSS as currently implemented may not be adequate to counteract this. Competitiveness was proposed by a majority of the selected interviewees as the preferred goal for regional policy, and it was suggested that a dedicated focus on the competitiveness of the growth centres in each region could, in time, deliver a degree of balanced growth across Ireland.

Investment planning was viewed by regional bodies as over-influenced by the sectoral priorities of government departments; there was a general view that new mechanisms are required to improve the territorial co-ordination of investment planning and the co-production of national and regional investment strategies. The study reaffirmed the need for an efficient regional transport network and for strategies at regional level to build regional research and innovation capacity. It also found a need for stricter planning enforcement as well as greater co-ordination of investment at growth centre level. Territorial governance arrangements were found to be weak, with no central unit of government responsible for the co-ordination of regional policy, and the regional tier of public administration was found to be functionally limited and under-utilised.

The study concludes that there has been limited prioritisation to date of investment in the designated gateways to create linked dynamic and attractive urban growth centres with sufficient critical mass to increase regional productivity. The regional governance arrangements and strategic capacity required to ensure the co-ordination and integration of investment are currently too weak to be effective.

Applying the policy coherence framework developed for this study, the conclusion is reached that regional policy in Ireland performs poorly in terms of both internal and external consistency, with deficiencies identified within many elements of the coherence framework.

Recommendations are made in relation to central government co-ordination, review of regional bodies, preparation of integrated regional strategies, regional innovation, benchmarking regional competitiveness, enforcement of regional planning guidelines, measurement of regional policy outcomes, prioritisation of public investment and regional proofing of sectoral strategies.

Utility of the study

This study is intended to make a contribution to the regional policy debate in Ireland. The strategic focus of Irish regional policy is once again largely determined by Irish policymakers, although it is still subject to some EU policy influences. A policy coherence framework has been developed that incorporates new understandings of the policy governance process, and this is utilised to provide new perspectives on the internal and external coherence of Irish regional policy.

A transdisciplinary approach was adopted, incorporating regional economics, economic geography and public policy governance, to undertake a detailed analysis of the Irish situation. This study provides new insights into the strategic investment and spatial planning processes and regional governance in Ireland. It also addresses the key question of how the potentially conflicting goals of territorial cohesion, polycentric urban development and competitiveness could be reconciled in an Irish context. Recommendations are made on how an effective territorial dimension can be introduced into the policy process, recognising that without adequate consideration of spatial effects, undifferentiated sectoral policies can aggravate regional economic disparities.

A coherent and strategic focus in relation to regional policy is beneficial for the development and prioritisation of investment policies, the development of appropriate governance models to lead and co-ordinate regional policy, and the adoption of appropriate benchmarks by which to measure progress towards the agreed goal(s).

Without a clear rationale and a robust framework in which regional policy planning and implementation can take place, there is a risk, according to Perry (2006), of advancing on the basis of suppositions, making investments to emulate perceived, rather than proven, best practice. This echoes Hutchcroft (2001: 46), who argues that if current territorial governance frameworks are to succeed, 'they must rest not merely on faith, but also on discerning analysis'. This study is intended to make a timely contribution towards such an analysis.

Structure

Chapter 1 having set the context and defined the approach adopted, Chapter 2 provides a theoretical orientation to the study in the areas of regional growth theories and regional policy and on the concept of policy coherence. It includes a review of the indicators commonly applied to determine regional economic growth and convergence/divergence. The influential concepts of territorial cohesion, polycentric development and regional competitiveness are described and their potential application to Irish regional policy is considered. The rationale for regional policy intervention and the principal instruments of regional economic policy, spatial planning and territorial governance are then set out. Finally, Chapter 2 provides a framework within which the concepts of policy coherence and policy effectiveness, as they apply to regional policy, can be understood.

The approach that was adopted to design and carry out the study is set out in Chapter 3. It commences with the philosophical stance that influenced the definition of the research issues, the methodological approach (research design) and the analysis and interpretation of the data. The design of the research instruments used, i.e. analysis of primary and secondary data sources and semi-structured interviews is described as well as the selection of research themes, with reference to the literature review and the specific research objectives defined. Finally, the methods used to gather, assimilate and interpret the data are described.

In Chapter 4, a range of primary and secondary documentary and statistical sources are reviewed. The chapter commences by tracing the evolution of regional policy in Ireland over recent decades and then critiques the salient features of the main investment programmes and selected sectoral strategies. It concludes with an analysis of the sources of regional disparities and an assessment of recent regional socioeconomic trends. This review informed the selection of interviewees and the questions to be addressed to the interviewees.

The findings of the semi-structured interviews are set out and discussed in Chapter 5 in the light of the insights derived from the literature review in Chapter 2. The findings are sequenced according to the interview guide used and are correlated, where applicable, with the findings of Chapter 4.

The concluding chapter draws together conclusions on the substantive issues addressed in this study with reference to the theoretical perspectives used. It summarises the findings in relation to the research questions and discusses the implications for regional economic and spatial planning and territorial governance within Ireland. Conclusions are also drawn on the utility of policy coherence as a policy analysis framework. Some recommendations arising from the conclusions are set out. Finally, the limitations of the research undertaken and some areas that merit further study are identified.

2

Regional Economic Growth and Regional Policy

The purpose of this chapter is to provide a theoretical orientation to the study of regional economic growth theories and regional policy and the concept of policy coherence. Regional economic growth theories, the principles underlying the influential concepts of cohesion, polycentric development and competitiveness, and alternative regional policy approaches are of particular interest in the context of regional policy. The review of existing knowledge in these areas also serves to identify some of the core dilemmas facing regional policy framers and to inform the critical review of Irish regional policy in Chapter 4 and the identification of the issues to be explored in the semi-structured interviews. The chapter concludes with a framework within which the concepts of policy coherence and policy effectiveness, as they apply to regional policy in Ireland, can be understood.

Regional economic growth theories

Much attention in recent years has been focused on the factors that drive regional and national economic growth rates and on how public policies can affect growth rates. An understanding of economic growth theories and the mechanisms that shape spatial economic growth can help to explain historical disparities in regional economies and guide the construction of appropriate regional policies (Armstrong and Taylor, 2000; Morgenroth, 2003a). Three alternative regional economic growth theories are reviewed in this section and their relevance to a study on Irish regional policy is considered.

Neoclassical growth theory

The neoclassical exogenous growth model, first pioneered by Solow (1956), suggests that output growth depends on growth in the level of capital per worker and the exogenous rate of technological progress (Gardiner et al., 2004). According to this growth theory, poor countries and regions should tend to grow faster than rich ones, independent of their starting point, due to free factor mobility and diminishing returns to capital (Hofer and Wörgöter, 1997). Interregional trade provides an equalising mechanism, as regions will specialize in and consequently export products that intensively utilize the factors of production in which they have a comparative advantage and that they possess in abundance (Angelis et al., 2006).

The neoclassical growth theory predicts that regional income disparities will be reduced over time in growing economies, due to the influence of technology on productivity (Pike et al., 2006). Accordingly, all that is required to attain convergence in factor incomes (wages and return on capital) between regions is to introduce policies to facilitate the free movement of labour, capital and goods (Bradley, 2005).

Within the neoclassical school, Williamson's (1965) 'spatial equilibrium' theory predicts that in the early stages of economic development, income inequality between regions will increase, largely because of rapid urbanisation. This will be followed by a period of economic stability, characterised by continued inequality between regions. Finally, a lessening of regional inequality will set in as the national economy matures and urban diseconomies take effect. Williamson's theory suggests that if cross-region spillovers are sufficiently strong, market forces alone can bring about a solution to regional inequality. A corollary of this is that financial transfers, applying minimum wage rates and unemployment insurance can exacerbate regional disparities by interfering with 'natural' capital and labour movements (Lipshitz, 1995).

Within the neoclassical theoretical framework, three distinct types of convergence activity have been postulated. First, unconditional convergence implies that poor regions grow faster than rich ones and all regions eventually converge to the same steady-state income levels (Herz, 2002). Second, conditional convergence predicts that to the extent that regions differ in their fundamental endowments, per capita output does converge to a long-run equilibrium state and that a regional economy that is furthest away from its own steady state will grow fastest (Herz, 2002). Whereas unconditional convergence would require that all economies be structurally identical, differing only in their initial conditions, conditional convergence relaxes the assumption of similar steady states. Third, there is the concept of the convergence club, i.e. a 'group of economies whose initial conditions are near enough to converge towards the same long term equilibrium' (Dall'erba and Le Gallo, 2003: 8). Quah (1996) found some evidence of 'twin peaks' or convergence clubs of rich and poor countries.

Some empirical evidence of convergence is to be found in longitudinal studies of convergence among EU Member States, and these are seen as supportive of the premise of neoclassical growth theory. However, as some of the underlying assumptions of the theory do not apply (i.e., free market, minimal intervention), such convergence cannot easily be ascribed to neoclassical growth processes. Barro and Sala-i-Martin (1995) demonstrated evidence in favour of the convergence hypothesis, albeit at a relatively modest rate (~2% per annum). Dall'erba and Le Gallo (2003) found evidence of greater cohesion among European countries, but increasing disparities among regions within countries. Similarly, Barry (2003) asserts that structural funds may have aided convergence with the EU average, but caused a widening of intra-state disparities. This phenomenon is not unique to Europe. In a study of territorial income inequalities in Canada, Alasai (2003) found that disparities between the Canadian provinces had declined but intra-province disparities had increased, indicating a trend towards spatial economic concentration and a worsening urban/rural divide.

The persistence of regional variations in economic performance within EU Member States would indicate that this theory does not fully capture the processes that are taking place. A frequent criticism of the theory is that it does not allow for the fact that regions differ in their fundamental conditions, e.g. physical capital and skills base, and that technological progress tends to be uneven (Pike et al., 2006). Gaps in economic welfare across regions may be preserved in the long term due to the differing steady states that exist across them, according to Boyle et al. (1999).

Neoclassical growth theory was challenged as early as 1957 by Gunder Myrdal, whose cumulative causation theory asserted that the operation of market forces would increase rather than decrease inequalities, due to the migration of both capital and labour to growing regions and as a result of regions' different economic starting points and resource endowments (Lipshitz, 1995). Many of the assumptions underlying the automatic convergence process predicted by the theory do not always apply, and the removal of barriers to factor movements may in some cases exacerbate economic disparities (Bradley, 2005).

A further critique of the neoclassical growth theory addresses its non-interventionist stance, which is in contrast to the underlying assumption of the endogenous and new economic geography theories that contend that regions do not converge in the absence of appropriate regional policies.

Endogenous growth theory

The endogenous growth model, first associated with Romer (1986), asserts that per-capita income is mainly influenced by region- or country-specific endogenous factors that influence the level of outputs (Brasili and Gutierrez, 2004). Endogenous growth theory focuses on how reproducible and mutually reinforcing factors such as infrastructure, human capital, sectoral specialisation, financial intermediation and social capital can accumulate, thus overcoming the limitations of diminishing returns (Morgenroth, 2003b). In the absence of technological catch-up, these growth models predict diverging regional incomes in the growth process (Herz, 2002). The reasons for this include the emergence of some regions as innovation leaders, the concentration of public and private investment in R&D in selected regions, and the non-linear patterns of innovation diffusion (Armstrong and Taylor, 2000). These leading regions become the sources of basic inventions and apply these locally, as technology spillovers tend to be localized and therefore the differences in productivity between regions widen over time (Gardiner et al., 2004).

It is acknowledged in the endogenous growth model that R&D and knowledge accumulation, i.e. the stock of human capital, drives technological progress and thus generates growth (Boyle et al., 1999). Human capital is considered important for two reasons: it determines a region's ability to absorb new technology and it is an important factor in determining a region's ability to generate its own technological progress. Thus, Armstrong and Taylor (2000: 87) suggest that:

> Knowledge-rich regions with an institutional environment conducive to the creation and transmission of new ideas will have a continuing advantage over less well endowed regions.

The endogenous growth theory also asserts that investment in public infrastructure can improve connectivity, expand market access and sustain growth, and that investment in productive firms further stimulates economic growth. Specialisation, market expansion and technological adaptation reinforce market dominance. Social capital matters because business environments with high levels of trust and effective institutional processes increase collaboration and interdependence between firms and are more conducive to investment (Graham and Hart, 1999; Morgenroth, 2003b).

Traditionally, comparative advantages were based on raw materials and factor endowments (i.e. labour and capital). In this new context, competitive advantage is based on endowments of human capital and local synergies, whereby management of change (innovation) and mobilisation at regional level are critical. In weakly institutionalised regions, this mobilisation is unlikely to occur. Similarly, peripheral, traditional industrial, rural and border regions, which all suffer from specific handicaps, are unlikely to converge with non-disadvantaged regions due to uneconomic firms, poor access infrastructure, low labour skills and poor capital markets (Armstrong and Taylor, 2000). Endogenous growth theory suggests that the emphasis of regional policy should be on enhancing the qualities and endowments of regions themselves, particularly knowledge capital and investment in R&D (Keating, 1997; Audretsch and Keilbach, 2004).

Endogenous growth theory thus provides a strong rationale for public investments that enhance the conditions for economic growth, such as public infrastructure, human capital, research and development and technology diffusion. It also accords an important role to the institutional environment that enables local synergies, social capital and effective regional governance.

Criticisms of endogenous growth theory include the fact that its prediction of divergence does not accord with the empirical evidence of (slight) convergence in some economic indicators, across the EU and within states, including Ireland. Al Ubeydli and Kealey (2000) state that it is incorrectly assumed that knowledge is freely available, whereas it has many of the features of a private good. Pike et al. (2006) state that the endogenous growth theory does not take sufficient account of how difficult it can be to overcome the constraints on development imposed by historical, social and institutional contexts. They state that patterns of underdevelopment can be locked in in some circumstances and that some regions may not respond to policies aimed at enhancing their endogenous potential.

New economic geography models

Not dissimilar to endogenous growth theory, the new economic geography models seek to explain how spatial patterns, i.e. agglomeration and dispersion of economic activity, come about. Among the pioneers of new economic geography are Fujita (1988), Krugman (1991) and Venables (1996).

These models, according to Gardiner et al. (2004: 1050):

> attribute regional differences in growth to localized increasing returns from the spatial agglomeration of specialized economic activity and the endogenous effects such localized specialization generates (accumulation of skilled labour, local knowledge spillovers, specialized suppliers and services etc).

What differentiates the new economic growth theories is the assumption that the marginal product of capital is constant and potentially increasing, rather than diminishing as in the neoclassical theories. Capital is understood to include investment in human capital, research and development and knowledge/skills, and creativity is considered an important driver of economic development. Agglomeration economies, according to Armstrong and Taylor (2000), arise from the geographical association of a large number of economic activities such as transport links, skilled labour, government services, legal and commercial services and financial services.

Significantly, the new economic geography theories predict a core–periphery equilibrium pattern of productivity, due to firms and populations agglomerating in larger 'growth' centres to avail of increasing returns to scale, reduced transport costs and the attraction of higher wages (Krugman, 1991). An agglomeration economy is defined by O'Leary (2007: 257) as 'an increase in the productivity or a decrease in the unit cost of a business, consequent on the concentration of economic activity at a given location'. One of the consequences of agglomeration economies is a 'brain-drain' from less developed areas to the more capital-intensive, technologically advanced growth centres. This process is often reinforced by the location decisions of foreign firms setting up in the growth centres.

The new economic geography models, similarly to endogenous growth theories, also predict that the knowledge spillovers from intellectual human capital will be spatially restricted, e.g. adjacent to research institutions. The new economic geography models accord an important role to infrastructure in fostering domestic firms and attracting inward investment and they predict that infrastructure investment will have its greatest impact in larger urban centres. Fujita (1988) demonstrated that pure market processes based on price interactions alone can generate spatial agglomeration of economic activities. Venables (1996) demonstrated that agglomeration of firms can be generated equally well arising from the interplay between the location decisions of firms, even where there is little or no labour mobility. Growth and agglomeration can thus be mutually reinforcing (Morgenroth, 2003a).

The new economic geography models cited above suggest that market forces generate economies of scale (both internal and external), thus intensifying the spatial concentration of economic activity, with capital migrating towards the centres of greatest return (Angelis et al., 2006). Such centres will, over time, become even stronger (cumulative effects) as centres of economic and political power. The periphery, in turn, benefits from the wealth that the dynamic of the core has created, but perpetually lags behind. In the light of agglomeration effects, grant-based incentives may be ineffective in countering the underlying forces that determine the most advantageous locations for industry and a growth node strategy may be more appropriate (Fitzgerald et al., 1999).

Drawing on the work of Pritchett (1996), Boyle et al. (1999) attribute agglomeration economies to increased industrial specialisation and sharing of specialised inputs, the presence of a 'thick' labour market and localised knowledge spillovers. Atherton and Johnston (2005) attribute location-specific economies of scale to firm-specific and industry-specific economies of agglomeration and to economies of urbanisation due to an increased variety of services and a larger proximate market. Agglomeration of firms facilitates information exchange and knowledge spillovers, thus enhancing innovation and also dynamic labour markets. Given these advantages, firms will be attracted to clusters of other firms with complementary areas of activity. In addition, the more intensive use of infrastructural assets by a larger number of firms raises overall productivity (OECD, 2005).

Atherton and Johnston (2005) predict that the phenomenon of major urban centres dominating economic activity will increase over time as firms seek competitive advantages. Fitzgerald et al. (2003) observe that different sectors have different tendencies to agglomerate, so that regions that provide conditions conducive to the growth of these sectors will benefit from faster growth rates. However, there are processes that limit and constrain agglomeration economies and contribute to the emergence of multiple settlements (Atherton and Johnson, 2005). These include land and rental cost increases due to the increased demand for limited space; congestion costs and travel time increases; and access to natural resources.

The concentration of economic activities in core cities and regions has significant economic, social and environmental implications for peripheral regions. In a critique of these models, Pike et al. (2006) highlight the models' reliance on mathematical formulae and their neglect of real social and cultural milieux. Pike et al. (2006: 109) criticise the models' failure to consider 'the influence of local institutional, social and cultural structures in facilitating or constraining local and regional development'. Referring to agglomeration and other processes, Commins (2006: 3) states that 'peripheral economies tend to be incorporated into international economic processes and relationships in terms that benefit the core regions more than the peripheries'.

Martin (2000: 1) describes spatial concentration of economic activities as 'one of the most salient features of economic development.' Martin also claims that the urge on the part of policymakers 'to counteract such a trend through public policies is also striking'. Atherton and Johnston (2005: 23) conclude that regional policy should recognise and support agglomeration as a beneficial economic phenomenon.

Relevance of regional economic growth theories to this study

Although the regional growth theories reviewed above offer contradictory evidence of regional growth and disparities, it is appropriate at this point to consider the relevance of the alternative growth theories to an empirical study such as this on improving the coherence of Irish regional policy.

The evident differences in historical resource endowments, existence of market failures and uneven rates of technological adaptation in Ireland suggest that the market adjustment mechanisms operating through free trade and labour and capital mobility, anticipated by the neoclassical growth model, are unlikely to operate adequately to bring about more balanced regional economic development, although there has been apparent convergence in labour market, demographic and disposable income indicators in recent years (further analysed in Chapter 4). Fitzgerald and Morgenroth (2006) cite Williamson's (1965) spatial equilibrium model, suggesting that spillovers from the more prosperous Dublin area may, over time, reduce regional disparities. O'Leary (2007) also suggests that trends in productivity growth in Irish regions may be following the process described by Williamson, but concludes that the question remains an open one, pending further research into the extent of increasing returns in Irish regions.

On the other hand, trends in regional productivity (gross value added (GVA) per capita) reveal persistent divergence, indicating that either the endogenous potential of some regions is greater than that of others or processes of cumulative causation or agglomeration are at work. Endogenous growth theory provides a strong rationale for public investments that enhance the conditions for economic growth and also for territorial governance systems at national and regional levels that enable effective co-ordination and mobilisation of regional resources. The move to endogenous economic development in response to the competitiveness challenge ordinarily shifts the focus for policy intervention from the national to the regional level, as suggested by Keating (2000). However, in spite of the economic efficiencies that may accrue from this and the potentially important institutional role of subnational authorities, this has not yet taken place to any great extent in Ireland (Morgenroth, 2000).

Boyle et al. (1999) suggested that the concentration of economic activity in Ireland reflects agglomeration economies that are important for productivity growth, but these are being offset by the negative effects of under-investment in transport infrastructure. They proposed that regional spaces in Ireland should be organised around strong urban centres with sufficient critical mass and that the only feasible way to elaborate a regional policy based on productivity is through the expansion of the commuting compass of strong urban centres. Fitzgerald and Morgenroth (2006) have also suggested that the empirical evidence for the existence of agglomeration effects in Ireland is quite strong.

Consideration of these alternative economic growth theories provides the theoretical underpinning for the focus of this study on public policy interventions that seek to alter economic geography – specifically through investment strategies and enhanced territorial governance (to unlock endogenous potential) – and on spatial structuring (to facilitate more balanced economic development). The research instruments used include an exploration of the causes of economic disparities in Ireland and on the appropriate policy approaches required to ameliorate these.

Measurement of regional performance and convergence

There is no universally accepted measure by which comparisons of regional economic performance and the extent of economic convergence across regions and states can be conducted. The principal measures applied are reviewed in this section.

GDP and income per capita

The most commonly used measure of regional output is GDP (gross domestic product) per capita. This is the principal measure used by the EU to determine eligibility for structural funds assistance. It is not without limitations, however. While regional GVA or GDP is a measure of the value of the goods and services produced in a region, it does not take account of where the ownership of the factors of production resides. In Ireland, for example, the extent of profit repatriations has meant that GDP exceeded GNP (gross national product) by approximately 15% at the end of the 1990s (Boyle et al., 1999; O'Leary, 1999). The unreliability of the conventional GVA per capita measure of regional output is highlighted by Fitzgerald and Morgenroth (2006) and by O'Leary (2007), both calling for more detailed regional analysis to determine a more accurate measure of regional output. A further problem noted by Boyle et al. (1999) is the high level of inter-regional commuting. Dall'erba and Le Gallo (2003: 14) refer to this as the modifiable areal unit problem.

A further critique of GDP offered by O'Hara et al. (2008) is that it is an explicitly economistic measure that does not capture overall societal wellbeing. The European Commission acknowledges the weaknesses inherent in using GDP per capita as the primary indicator in assessing levels of economic development, citing the inter-regional commuting effect and the exclusion of transfers, but concludes that 'by common assent it is the best measure available' (CEC, 2004a: 25).

Disposable household income per capita is perhaps a better measure of welfare as it includes all gross financial receipts and state transfer payments, less direct taxation. Differences between the gaps in GVA per capita and disposable income per capita derive from three sources. First, welfare payments are made to the retired and unemployed, who do not contribute directly to output. Second, commuting affects the figures, as income is measured at place of residence and output at place of work. Third, transfer pricing and profit shifting by foreign-owned firms biases GVA figures upwards (Fitzgerald et al., 2003). The apparent equalising effect of using income transfers is critiqued by O'Hara et al. (2008), who state that reliance on such transfers does not tackle underlying structural deficiencies in weaker regions or promote productivity convergence.

O'Leary (1999) suggests adjusting regional GVA for net factor outflows[2] by adjusting regional output figures for the estimated level of profit outflows, thus yielding a more accurate regional income (equivalent to GNP) estimate for Irish regions. This method yields regional income figures 15% lower on average than regional GVA, leading O'Leary to argue that regional income is a more accurate measure than regional GVA.

Convergence

Convergence ordinarily implies a negative correlation between a region's level of per capita income and its average growth rate. Three broad concepts of convergence can be distinguished: β-convergence, σ-convergence and γ-convergence (Hofer and Wörgöter, 1997).

The spatial level at which cohesion and convergence are assessed is significant (Hofer and Wörgöter, 1997; Casellas & Galley, 1999; Walsh, 2005). For example, Casellas and Galley (1999) claim that the NUTS classification framework used by the EU is not sufficiently coherent due to the heterogeneity of European regions within each category and demonstrated that by merging city regions with their hinterlands, the apparent level of disparities was reduced.

β-Convergence

Dall'erba and Le Gallo (2003: 8) describe the β-convergence hypothesis, which predicts that 'the growth rate of a region is positively related to the distance that separates it from its steady state'. According to Boyle et al. (1999), the degree of regional convergence can be established by regressing the growth in GDP per capita on the initial level of GDP per capita. This is known as Barro regressions or tests of β-convergence. If the result of the regressions is statistically significant, then it can be concluded that the poorer regions are growing faster than the richer ones. Dall'erba and Le Gallo (2003: 10) cite several criticisms of the use of β-convergence, including 'heterogenous patterns of economic development over space'.

σ-Convergence

The concept of σ-convergence refers to a reduction in the cross-sectional dispersion of per capita income across a group of regions over time

2 Net factor outflows are calculated based on profit outflows, interest paid on foreign-held debt, profit inflows from Irish multinationals and employee remittances from abroad.

(Giannias et al., 1999). The measurement of σ-convergence involves the calculation of the coefficient of variation of cross-regional measures of economic welfare over time (Boyle et al., 1999). Coefficient of variation has been widely used to measure temporal variations in the regional distribution of income.

γ-Convergence

In order to overcome the problem identified by Sala-i-Martin (1994) that the absence of σ-convergence does not imply the absence of β-convergence, Boyle et al. (1999) apply an index of rank concordance (to capture the extent of intra-distributional mobility), which they term γ-convergence, in conjunction with the index of σ-convergence in order to determine whether β-convergence exists in a situation where σ-convergence is constant.

Measurement: Conclusions

Consistent and reliable measurement of regional economic output is an important policy tool, but this is problematic in an Irish context due to the effects of profit repatriation by multinationals based here. A more accurate measure of regional income is needed to take account of this as well as regular measures of comparative regional performance. The issue of measurement has therefore been included as one of the research themes for this study.

Influential concepts: Territorial cohesion, polycentric urban development and competitiveness

In the recent literature on regional development, three influential concepts can be discerned: territorial cohesion, polycentric urban development and regional competitiveness. Although EU cohesion policy marshals all three in support of its strategic orientation, there are tensions among them and each implies distinctive approaches to regional investment policy.

The principal features of each of these concepts, which are important drivers of regional policy, are described in the following subsections. This is followed by consideration of how they may be reconciled in practice in Ireland.

Territorial cohesion

The overarching goals of economic and social cohesion and, latterly, territorial cohesion have found their clearest expression in EU cohesion policy and it is in this context that the concept of territorial cohesion is considered. Article 2 of the Treaty on European Union specifies that the community mission will be to 'promote economic and social progress and a high level of employment and to achieve balanced sustainable development … through the strengthening of economic and social cohesion' (CEC, 2004a: 27).

Territorial cohesion, although it has no formal definition, is described by the EU Commission (CEC, 2004a: 3) as 'the balanced distribution of human activities across the Union' and as complementary to economic and social cohesion, translating the objective of balanced development into spatial terms. It can be defined somewhat simplistically as 'no region left behind'. It also involves building on each region's strengths in order to better contribute to the overall goal of competitiveness. The EU's territorial agenda is therefore related to the Lisbon process and seeks more coherent approaches to territorial development (CEC, 2006b: 2).

The essence of territorial cohesion, according to Faludi (2006), is that people should not be disadvantaged by where they live and work in the EU. Faludi traces the origins of territorial cohesion to the French concept of *aménagement du territoire*, which involves the effective management of the entire territory, rebalancing of the economy, an emphasis on national–regional–local partnership and promotion of endogenous development, and the maintenance of (potentially unviable) services of general interest.

Several writers have noted that in the concept of territorial cohesion, the EU is attempting to reconcile the potentially incompatible objectives of external competitiveness and internal cohesion and the twin challenges of convergence and cohesion (Glen, 2002; Commins, 2006). Glen (2002: 7) defines convergence as 'harmonisation of macro-economic indicators' and cohesion as 'raising living standards for all'. The EU Commission considers territorial cohesion an essential precondition for the economic and political success of the building of the European Community, and acknowledges that the recent economic convergence achieved between Member States has been accompanied by an exacerbation of disparities and asymmetries within those states (CEC, 2004a: 8). The European Commission sees territorial cohesion and polycentric development as two key concepts relating to balanced development. However, the absence of a clear meaning and interpretation leaves scope for different applications of the policy in different Member States (Bachtler and Wishlade, 2004).

Structural funds are the most important element of EU cohesion policy, accounting for a large portion of the EU budget, with over 70% targeted at the least developed regions. The EU also has an important policy co-ordination and harmonisation function; for example, agriculture, rural, competition and trade policies play a significant role in 'transforming the underlying structures and competitiveness of the weaker beneficiary economies' (Bradley, 2005: 2). Cohesion policy is sometimes considered as a counterbalance to the likely effect of economic integration on exacerbating core–periphery disparities in Europe. In the context of this study, it is noteworthy that the need for policy consistency and co-ordination across different policies, in order to promote synergies and maximise policy coherence at regional level, has been recognised by the EU (CEC, 2004a).

The EU's cohesion policy also plays a significant role in triggering institutional, process and policy adaptations at national level; this is evident in the translation of EU regional policy into domestic policies over time (Laffan, 2004: 2). Cohesion policy for the 2007–13 period has been refocused on the contribution to the EU's growth and jobs strategy in line with the renewed Lisbon agenda, and the Community Strategic Guidelines (CEC, 2006a) for this period accord cohesion policy a central role in the attainment of the EU's ambitions. From an Irish perspective, the emphasis of the regional competitiveness and employment (Objective 2) programmes is on anticipating and promoting economic change. A further development has been the publication of a communication on the contribution of urban areas to growth and jobs in the EU's regions (CEC, 2006b).

Territorial cohesion, although lacking a precise definition, is an influential overarching goal of EU regional policy. In its Green Paper on Territorial Cohesion, the European Commission (2008) has sought to develop a clearer understanding of the concept and this is a positive development, as fuzzy concepts do not provide clear policy direction. Public investment in Ireland has been highly contingent on EU regional and cohesion funding for almost two decades, but the extent of this is much reduced from 2007 onwards.

Polycentric urban development

The value of spatial planning in providing frameworks to guide physical development and the co-ordination of investment decisions is increasingly being recognised. Polycentric urban development exists when proximate urban centres develop in a complementary manner, exhibiting functional co-operation and specialisations, thus supporting a larger conjoined functional area and acting in many respects like a larger urban centre (Department of the Environment, Heritage and Local Government (DEHLG), 2006). According to the European Spatial Planning Observatory Network (ESPON, 2004), polycentricity strengthens regional competitiveness and is considered a desirable counterbalance to monocentricity (a single dominant city) and urban sprawl. To achieve polycentricity requires a high level of connectivity, consensus-building and co-ordination, and this poses new challenges in terms of inter-institutional networking and the identification of shared investment priorities. These are much more difficult to achieve in dispersed peripheral regions (ESPON, 2004).

The European Spatial Development Perspective (ESDP), agreed in 1999, provided an impetus to strategic spatial planning (Walsh, 2005). According to the ESDP, polycentric spatial planning can avoid increases in regional disparities through the promotion of a more even distribution of growth; well-balanced regional labour markets; reduction of pressure on transport infrastructure; and balanced and sustainable development. The overarching objective of the ESDP is to 'achieve a balanced and sustainable development of the territory of the EU' (CEC, 1999: 10). The ESDP calls for the creation of a network of internationally accessible metropolitan regions and their linked hinterlands in order to achieve a stronger integration of EU regions into the global economy. It recognises the functional interdependencies between cities and their surrounding countryside and it highlights the need for dynamic, attractive and competitive cities with sufficient economic potential, critical mass and a diversified economic base (CEC, 1999). From a territorial governance perspective, the ESDP calls for closer co-operation between the authorities responsible for sectoral policies and those responsible for spatial development, at each horizontal level, and states that the application of the ESDP is the responsibility of both sectoral and spatial planning authorities.

There have been several claims that the concept of polycentric urban development is vague and unproven, at best providing a guiding framework (Parr, 2005a; Ward, 2008). Parr (2005a) suggests that polycentric urban development should not be a regional policy goal in itself but a means to achieve regional policy goals, and questions the excessive reliance on the concept to deliver economic and social cohesion in the EU. Walsh (2005) identifies some apparent contradictory goals in the ESDP such as the concept of 'balanced competitiveness' and 'polycentric urban networks', which he claims could apply at several spatial scales with potentially contradictory outcomes.

A further critique of polycentric urban development is offered by Weith and Zillmer (2006) and by Ward (2008), who stress the potentially negative implications of promoting polycentric urban development for the development of peripheral rural regions and the weakly urbanised areas between the growth poles. Weith and Zillmer (2006) predict that defining the role of the 'regions in between' solely in terms of their relationship to, or dependence on, the metropolitan regions, or in terms of producing non-commodity public goods, e.g. cultural and recreational landscapes, is a recipe for deepening intra-regional disparities. These concerns can be overcome to some extent by a strengthening of urban–rural linkages and by promoting distinctive growth strategies for rural areas so that interdependent urban and rural areas can mutually benefit from economic development.

Ward (2008) describes the concept as excessively economistic and one that reinforces outdated notions of centrality and hierarchy. Ward also expresses concerns that the privileging of city-region strategies is having a deterministic influence on regional development planning and investment and, consequently, on patterns of economic development. These concerns reflect those of Pike et al. (2006), who state that broader notions of the quality of places and concerns for sustainability are required, reflecting new emphases on ecological modernisation and the localisation of production and consumption patterns.

The underlying principles of polycentric urban development as set out in the ESDP are clearly evident in the Irish National Spatial Strategy (NSS), published by the DEHLG in 2002, and in particular in the more recent Atlantic Gateways initiative, which sets out a strategy for linking the designated gateways along the western and south-western seaboard (DEHLG, 2006). A critical synthesis of the NSS is provided in Chapter 4.

Regional competitiveness

The concept of regional competitiveness, like that of polycentric urban development, is gaining increased attention from policymakers. Regional competitiveness is recognised as an important contributor to national economic growth (Gardiner et al., 2004). According to Martin (2003: 2):

> A better understanding of the concept and the forces that drive it, will contribute in turn to a better understanding of the driving factors behind improving economic well-being and the geographic distribution of wealth.

Regional competitiveness takes on a further relevance in the context of the EU's competitiveness and employment objective, and the renewed Lisbon Agenda (2005) emphasised the critical role of regions in enhancing competitiveness, innovation performance and employment creation.

As distinct from macroeconomic competitiveness, which generally denotes a country or region that produces goods and services that meet the test of external competition, with high and rising living standards, regional competitiveness can be considered as the aggregate of firm competitiveness at region level, while also taking account of additional common assets that affect the competitiveness of firms located there. Martin (2003: 35) asserts that:

> The competitiveness of a region resides both in the competitiveness of its constituent individual firms and their interactions and in the wider assets and social, economic, institutional and public attributes of the region itself.

The pyramid model of regional competitiveness developed by Gardiner et al. (2004) highlights basic attributes, including the extent of strategic autonomy enjoyed by a region, as important conditions for regional competitiveness. There is a high degree of conformity between studies that seek to identify the primary factors that drive regional competitiveness, as identified by Walsh (2006). These include innovation in organisations, human capital, connectivity infrastructure, economic diversity and strategic capacity. The Expert Group on Future Skills Needs in Ireland (EGFSN, 2006: 44) considers that the attractiveness of a region for key growth sector companies is determined by 'the extent to which a region's capabilities and competencies meet the requirements of firms'.

According to the Forfás[3] *Annual Competitiveness Report* (2004: 3), nations and regions compete to 'capture the economic benefits available from high value industries by seeking to ensure that such industries locate and develop within their jurisdiction'. These activities tend to converge to a relatively small number of regions that provide access to the right skills, services and business environment. Regions must therefore compete to develop a 'winning formula' to attract companies in targeted high-growth sectors.

Within the field of economic geography, Martin (2003: 15) presents three conceptions of regional competitiveness:

- regions as sites of export specialisation – gaining competitive advantage through the exploitation of key locational endowments that enable regions to grow their export base
- regions as sources of increasing returns – endogenised technological change and enhanced human capital give rise to non-diminishing returns to scale
- regions as hubs of knowledge – specialised knowledge accumulates in a supportive institutional environment to secure regional economic advantage.

The economic wellbeing of regions and their inhabitants is increasingly dependent on their capacity to compete and succeed in the global marketplace. According to Gardiner et al. (2004: 1046):

> Regions and cities have no option but to strive to be competitive in order to survive in the new global marketplace and the new competition being forged by the new information or knowledge-driven economy.

3 Forfás is Ireland's national policy and advisory board for enterprise, trade, science, technology and innovation, operating under the auspices of the Department of Enterprise, Trade and Innovation.

Keating (2000: 143) terms this the 'competitiveness imperative', requiring regions to equip themselves with the assets, both tangible and intangible, along with foreign investment-friendly policies in order to maximise their attractiveness to global economic concerns. The rapid pace of change in technology necessitates ongoing investment in research and technology transfer and in the up-skilling of the labour force.

Adams et al. (2003: 19) caution against the use of regional competitiveness as a yardstick for comparison purposes, claiming that it implies winners and losers and that the 'cult of competitiveness' could lead to bad public policy due to wasteful competition between regions for footloose inward investment. A further critique of the notion of competitive advantage is that there is insufficient emphasis on collaborative advantage, which implies that regional institutions must be prepared to engage in multilateral networks through which to co-ordinate policy choices and address challenges of common concern.

Promoting national growth and competitiveness as a priority does not necessarily contribute to enhanced regional competitiveness. An exclusive focus on national growth may lead to a concentration of productive investment in 'winning regions' and a further weakening of weaker regions. O'Leary (2003) spells out cogent economic arguments in favour of an emphasis on regional competitiveness in Ireland, arguing that such an approach provides a basis for a more effective regional and national development policy. This would require that for each economic region there would be a prioritised investment programme and institutional reform aimed at unlocking its potential and enhancing its competitiveness. This is echoed by the National Economic and Social Council[4] (NESC, 2008), which acknowledges that regions will increasingly account for national economic prosperity and that regional policy has shifted from being redistributive to being constitutive of national economic wellbeing.

Reconciling the three concepts

The preceding subsections have considered the features of the three influential concepts of cohesion, polycentric development and competitiveness, as separate and distinct. It has been noted that none of the concepts has a universally accepted definition and they are prone to multiple alternative understandings and interpretations. Consequently, tensions can arise between them in relation to the determination of overarching policy goals and the spatial articulation of investment strategies. On the other hand, they do have

4 The function of the National Economic and Social Council is to report to the Taoiseach (Prime Minister) on strategic issues relating to the efficient development of the economy and social justice and the negotiation of agreements with the social partners.

complementary elements, and regional policy approaches can in practice seek to combine these elements.

Single-focus central policies, such as an exclusive emphasis on spatial or sectoral considerations, tend to yield unsatisfactory results (Parr, 2001). A sole concern with competitiveness could entail a concentration of investment in a small number of attractive cities and thus widen regional disparities. Adopting a spatial planning framework on its own would provide a hierarchical planning framework, but it would be ineffective without being linked to investment and there is a risk that too many growth centres would be selected, thus dissipating the benefits of concentrating growth. This would also compromise the ability of key regional locations to 'provide an environment in which internationally competitive industry may be embedded in Ireland's regional economies' (O'Leary, 2002). A focus on economic and social cohesion exclusively would entail higher investment in underperforming regions in order to reduce disparities, but is likely to be inefficient, as the aggregate economic benefits tend to be greater if investment is focused on sectors and in regions with the greatest growth potential.

In practice, these competing concepts can be somewhat reconciled. The mobilisation and exploitation of under-utilised potential in developing regions can contribute to improved competitiveness. Combining considerations of competitiveness and equity yields a form of 'balanced competitiveness' that would seek to combine a reduction in disparities with the stimulation of aggregate growth. This may not be optimal spatially if it doesn't operate within a clear spatial framework. The Irish NDP 2000–2006 (reviewed in Chapter 4) could be considered to fall into this category.

Combining the goals of cohesion with spatial planning in order to raise the potential of all regions should give rise to a more balanced settlement pattern, but may be economically inefficient by not maximising aggregate welfare, with investment being targeted at too many areas that do not maximise returns. The NSS 2002–2020, which lacked a coherent investment strategy, to some extent fits into this category with its apparent emphasis on distribution across several gateways and hubs rather than on growth and competitiveness.

Combining the objectives of polycentric development and competitiveness would give rise to a focusing of investment in urban centres as drivers of competitiveness; however, without consideration of the unequal potential of city regions, and the weak urban structure of some regions, uneven patterns of development could result. The Irish NDP 2007–13 would appear to be in this category, reflecting O'Leary's (2007: 264) view that policymakers now have 'a revealed preference for growth rather than regional balance'.

The optimal policy approach (presented diagrammatically in Figure 2.1) could be termed 'balanced efficiency', in which considerations of territorial cohesion, balanced competitiveness and urban-led growth are reconciled. In such a scenario, spatial equity, urban hierarchy or national growth do not predominate as the overarching goal of economic policy and planning. The implementation of the NDP 2007–13 within the framework of the NSS could potentially, if properly applied, provide such an optimal solution in which the co-ordinated investment in the designated growth centres leads to an enhancement of, and some convergence in, the productive capacity and attractiveness of the gateway regions. However, the differing scales of the gateways relative to each other and to Dublin would render this an aspirational objective within the seven-year term of the current NDP.

Figure 2.1: Overlapping concepts of cohesion, polycentric urban development and competitiveness

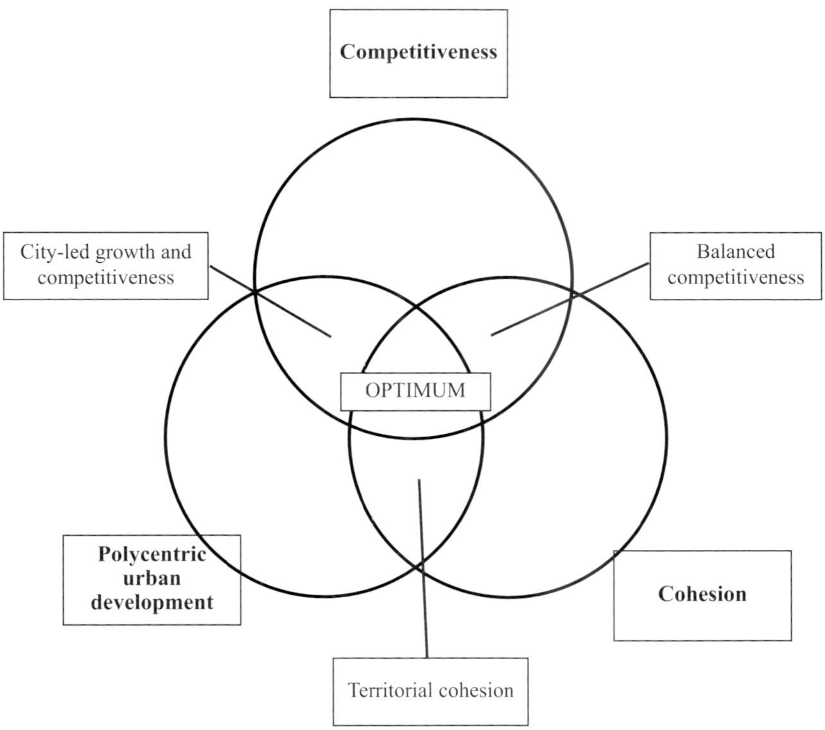

Do regions matter? The case for regional policy

The regional economics and regional policy literature contains abundant references to the rationale for states to introduce explicit regional policies. O'Hara and Commins (2003: 32) identify the fundamental sets of reasons as socio-political (equity) and market-economic (efficiency). Equity considerations concern the provision of minimum standards of public services, addressing spatial concentrations of social exclusion and the transfer of resources to improve economic opportunities and welfare (O'Hara and Commins, 2003). Inequities in the distribution of income underpin most of the social arguments for regional policy (Armstrong and Taylor, 2000). Market-economic considerations, on the other hand, justify regional policy on the basis of the need to overcome market failures and to invest in order to enhance regional potential, thus increasing aggregate national welfare (Morgenroth, 2000; O'Hara and Commins, 2003). The market economic system without intervention – operating through cumulative processes including the out-migration of the more highly skilled and mobile inhabitants – exacerbates territorial inequalities, thus necessitating a modification of the neoclassical approach and the introduction of policies that enable less developed regions to develop (Morgenroth, 2000).

Many commentators argue that an effective regional policy, tailored to raising the economic potential of all regions, is beneficial to the national economy and that unbalanced economic growth can undermine national economic performance in terms of employment and economic growth (Fitzgerald et al., 1999; Armstrong and Taylor, 2000; O'Leary, 2003; Adams et al., 2003; OECD, 2005; EGFSN, 2006). O'Leary (2003) argues that underperforming regions constrain national economic growth prospects and that regional policies based on regional competitiveness and innovation would offer the best guarantee of national competitiveness in the long run. This is supported by Gardiner et al. (2004: 1046) who refer to the 'regional foundations' of national competitiveness and advocate the development of new policy interventions to improve the competitiveness of each region and hence the national economy as a whole.

A further argument in favour of government intervention in regional policy is that it addresses allocative inefficiencies such as regional concentrations of unemployment, thus ameliorating income disparities and promoting economic development (Morgenroth, 2000; Glen, 2002; EGFSN, 2006). Martin (2000) points out that the location of economic activity affects the welfare of immobile workers and that low inter-sectoral mobility adds to the welfare cost of spatial concentration. He argues that some market failures are modified by the introduction of spatial considerations and that distance itself can be the source of market failures. Martin states that technological spillovers are spatially localised and that immobile workers and consumers in poorer regions suffer negative externalities due to the relocation of firms to richer regions. He cites the existence of imperfect competition in poorer regions, and states that investment to reduce transaction costs reduces the monopolistic power of local producers.

Government intervention also brings under-utilised regional resources into production, enhances the efficient use of social infrastructure and prevents sub-optimal resource allocation and resource inefficiency (Armstrong and Taylor, 2000; Glen, 2002; O'Hara and Commins, 2003). Unbalanced growth can lead to a self-perpetuating spiral of government investment to relieve congestion in the most economically advanced regions in the short to medium term, which stimulates further demand in the long term, rather than focusing on making lagging regions more economically attractive.

Morgenroth (2000: 4) states that 'there are particular growth benefits to be gained through the development of infrastructure, research and development and human capital which create externalities that have long-run positive impacts on the growth rate of a region/country'. In cases where the infrastructure deficit is quite large, investment in underdeveloped regions serves to increase the economic effectiveness of the infrastructure stock and is unlikely to give rise to diminishing returns in the same way as investment in already developed infrastructure networks (Bradley, 2005).

Reducing regional disparities is also important for improving the life chances, economic opportunities and quality of life of individuals (Adams et al., 2003). Balanced regional development is not simply about stimulating economic growth, but is ultimately about the wellbeing of the people who live and work in the regions and ensuring that they can have a better quality of life. This includes access to high-quality physical infrastructure as well as a range of other supports, services and facilities. Sharp disparities can undermine national solidarity and the sense of cohesion that create a national polity, thus policies that dispel disparities in incomes and unemployment rates are necessary (Adams et al., 2003).

There is also a strong rationale for regional policy at EU level in recognition of the likely impact of economic integration on Europe's lagging regions. The case for corrective policy interventions is made by the EU Commission in its Third Cohesion Report:

> the cost of not pursuing a vigorous cohesion policy to tackle disparities is, therefore, measured not only in terms of a loss of personal and social well-being but also in economic terms, in a loss of the potential real income and higher living standards. (CEC, 2004a: v)

The Third Cohesion Report established the reduction of disparities as the main goal of cohesion policy, and highlighted the importance of fostering economic development in all regions in order to enhance the competitiveness of the EU as a whole. There is also a strong correlation and complementarity between regional and agri-rural policy. Due to the ongoing reforms of agriculture policy, a strong regional economy is considered essential for the continued socioeconomic survival of rural communities.

The case for regional policy is not unequivocal. For example, both NESC (1997) and Martin (2000) refer to the trade-off between equity and efficiency arising when incentives to firms to locate in poorer regions reduce the efficiency of the overall economy and potentially reduce the resources available for further investment and redistribution. NESC (1997) suggests that redistribution between individuals may be more effective. A targeted, people-centred approach (e.g. training and employment measures), rather than a place-centred approach, to overcome regional income disparities is also advocated by Parr (2005a). This is echoed by Morgenroth (2000), who cautions against an overemphasis on economic dispersion, which he states must be gauged against the positive benefits of agglomeration and the clustering of firms.

Martin (2000) concludes that public policy aimed at altering economic geography, i.e. regional policy, can have multiple and contradictory effects. He states that policies that alter transaction costs, innovation and mobility of factors of production will change the location decisions of firms. Martin also argues that if agglomeration is a self-perpetuating mechanism, temporary subsidies will not alter the stability of the equilibrium. He makes an important distinction between policies aimed at improving the welfare of all regions (regional development) and policies aimed at narrowing inequalities (balanced regional development) (Martin, 2000: 10).

Notwithstanding the cogent arguments proffered in support of regional policy, the latter points do leave open the question of both the rationale and the focus of regional policy in Ireland. These are among the key research questions that are addressed in this study.

A typology of regional policies

Following from the previous section, this section provides an overview of the types of regional policies that are pursued by governments. Consistent with the three dimensions of regional policy that are the focus of this study, the policy approaches reviewed can be classified as investment-based approaches, governance-based approaches and spatial planning approaches. Each policy approach can be seen to draw its rationale from economic growth theories, economic geography or governance theories. In each case, the potential of the policy approach to build the productive capacity of underdeveloped regions and to narrow disparities is considered.

The political rationale for regionalisation has been shifting in recent decades from a protectionist style of regionalism emphasising consolidation of regional identity to one that embraces the opportunities presented by the new global environment. There have also been a number of macro-historic shifts in the underlying conceptualisation of regional policy. First, there was a shift from exogenous Keynesian resource transfers, in which the main players were often national agencies, to the stimulation of regional endogenous potential, for which the administrative loci are usually at regional level. Regions are no longer perceived as receptacles of regional policies imposed from above, but as contributors to overall national wellbeing. In this conception, regions no longer compete for limited resources as compensation for underdevelopment; rather, they negotiate strategically based on their contribution to national goals through the mobilisation of under-utilised potential. Second, the focus on EU-inspired regional policy is currently shifting to new regional policy approaches designed nationally (Ansell, 2000; O'Hara and Commins, 2003). Third, there has been what Commins (2006: 5) terms an 'economisation of regional policy' and a shift from a redistributive focus to a market-based focus reflecting the emergent predominance of competitiveness as a policy driver.

Distinct from these shifting approaches, O'Hara and Commins (2003: 53) identify what they term 'functional regionalism', whereby policies are conceived nationally but delivered regionally, with inadequate regional differentiation. In this scenario, the institutional capacity of region-level authorities remains circumscribed (Ansell, 2000).

Notwithstanding the changing emphases and rationales for regional policy intervention referred to above, aspects of each of the policies reviewed here are currently evident in Irish public policy. How these policies are deployed and their differential regional impacts depend largely on the interplay of national and regional policy objectives.

Promotion of labour and capital mobility

Neoclassical growth theories suggest that economic convergence can be achieved, provided that there is uninhibited labour and capital mobility and an enhancement of inter-regional trade, suggesting a minimisation of interventionist policies (Angelis et al., 2006). In a perfect market, capital and labour flows between regions would ensure the elimination of regional wage and unemployment rate disparities. Policies to enhance labour mobility can include retraining, housing supports, provision of Job Centres and flexible pension plans. Capital mobility into regional locations can be enhanced through tax and subsidy policies, enhancement of capital markets through loan guarantees, venture funds, implementation of location controls and incentives and the stimulation of indigenous social enterprises. The deliberate relaxation of business regulations to entice investment has been applied by US States, but is nascent in EU regional policy (Armstrong and Taylor, 2000).

However, neither labour nor capital is perfectly mobile. Inflexible wage levels that do not reflect productivity can impede labour mobility and erode the competitive position of regions, thus preventing market forces from narrowing income disparities (Afxentiou and Serletis, 1998; OECD, 2005). Socio-cultural factors such as risk aversion or social ties may also impede mobility (OECD, 2005). Capital will ordinarily be attracted to regions that can consistently generate high returns. The lack of dynamism in the economies of underdeveloped regions can give rise to a market failure due to the self-reinforcing patterns of market neglect (Keane and Garvey, 2006).

The Expert Group on Future Skills Needs (EGFSN, 2006) suggests that in a country the size of Ireland, normal labour market adjustments across regions should correct any imbalances in regional skills surpluses or deficits. However, the EGFSN identifies the need for improved transport communications to facilitate commuting and the availability of high-quality public services and amenities to meet the lifestyle expectations of a high-quality workforce in all regions.

Basing regional policy solely on an expectation of labour and capital mobility would appear to be a limited and almost certainly unsuccessful approach on its own, particularly if a region scores poorly on basic economic and social indicators, as suggested by Angelis et al. (2006). Nevertheless, policies designed to enhance labour and capital mobility continue to be used as instruments of regional policy.

Foreign direct investment

Attracting foreign direct investment (FDI) plays a substantial part in the economic development strategies of developing economies. Two principal rationales underpin FDI from the perspective of multinational corporations: to better serve a local market, and to improve operational effectiveness (Martin, 2003). Region-based attributes such as market access, transport infrastructure, favourable labour market conditions, promotional incentives, taxation rates and industrial structure are considered important 'pull' factors. The pull of existing firms in the same industrial sector, to avail of agglomeration and localisation economies, is also noted. The impact of FDI on a region's economy can depend on the extent to which it becomes embedded, with a high degree of linkages to local firms, leading to self-sustained expansion and clustering effects (Armstrong and Taylor, 2000).

FDI is recognised by the European Commission (CEC, 2004a) as playing a role in regional development, both as a source of new investment and employment and as a conduit for the introduction of high-value economic activities. However, as noted by the European Commission, foreign investors tend to be attracted to the best endowed rather than the weakest regions and tend to locate adjacent to large cities. In an era of globalisation and in the context of restrictions on regional aid rates imposed by EU state aid law, there are limits on the use of preferential regional incentives to stimulate investment in underdeveloped regions. Investors may also shift to locations outside the state if there are inadequate incentives in their preferred location within the state, resulting in a loss to the state as a whole (Morgan, 2002).

Perhaps as a result of Ireland's relatively peripheral location, successive Irish governments have adopted a strong policy emphasis on promoting external trade and inward investment. The A.T. Kearney Globalisation Index ranked Ireland as the world's fourth most globalised state in 2006, and FDI peaked at €30.8bn in 2002 (Forfás, 2005). In Ireland, as elsewhere, much of the inward investment has gone to the more prosperous areas, prompting the Industrial Development Authority (IDA) to set itself a target in 2000 of attracting 50% of greenfield job creation to the Border, Midland and Western (Objective 1) region, in order to rebalance the geographic spread of new developments. This target was never reached, and was dropped in 2007.

The attraction and embedding of FDI can greatly improve regional competitiveness. However, as noted above, foreign investors tend to cluster in and around large urban centres to avail of economies of agglomeration and localisation. Although FDI into Ireland appears to have peaked in 2002, attracting FDI is still a potent instrument of regional policy, reinforcing the need to increase the attractiveness and scale of the growth centres in order to ensure a more balanced spatial spread of high-value economic activity.

Development of indigenous enterprises

Promotion of indigenous enterprise development, via the stimulation of new firm formation and the expansion of existing firms, is a common strand of regional policy. New firm formation is driven by the fragmentation of larger firms, specialisation of business services, and opportunities for niche suppliers.

There are two distinct types of indigenous enterprise that can be promoted, namely small-scale locally based enterprises and high-technology competitive enterprises (Commins, 2006). Promotion of small-scale locally based enterprise, according to Commins (2006: 8), requires a decentralised, flexible, proactive approach in order to bring forward the 'latent potential' of products with a local character, e.g. speciality tourism, crafts, artisan foods and the provision of local services. Promotion of high-technology competitive enterprises, on the other hand, requires the building of research and innovation capabilities, identification and support for high-potential start-ups and an emphasis on globally competitive added-value products and services. It also involves the creation of an innovation milieu, whereby knowledge generation and application can occur (Commins, 2006). Geographical clusters of specialised firms are becoming an important dimension of regional economic development. High-technology industries show a clear tendency to form spatial clusters, characterised by spatial concentration and sectoral specialisation, supportive socio-cultural systems and an intense set of linkages and interdependencies. These confer positive external economies and require a strong network of supportive institutions and agencies (Armstrong and Taylor, 2000).

There is a positive correlation between rates of new firm formation/ expansion and reduction in regional income disparities (Armstrong and Taylor, 2000). The start-up and growth rates of small and medium-sized enterprises (SMEs) tend to be higher in more prosperous areas with higher population densities and a strong presence of working-age people, particularly with better education levels. Inner-city and peripheral areas generally perform poorly in terms of start-up rates (Armstrong and Taylor, 2000; Adams et al., 2003). The audit of innovation commissioned by the BMW Regional Assembly (CIRCA, 2004) confirmed that the entrepreneurship rates in the BMW region significantly lagged those in the Southern and Eastern region.

Audretsch and Keilbach (2004: 950) suggest that entrepreneurial capital, i.e. 'the capacity to harness new ideas by creating new enterprises', is a key factor that has been omitted from the traditional neoclassical production function. The determinants of entrepreneurship capital are shaped by legal, institutional and socio-cultural factors including a region's endowment with risk-taking entrepreneurs, a regulatory environment conducive to business start-up, 'thick' supportive networks, cultural acceptance of entrepreneurial activity, and the presence of sources of risk capital (Audretsch and Keilbach, 2004). Entrepreneurship stimulates economic output through the appropriation of knowledge spillovers in new enterprises and by increasing competition and the variety of enterprises in a region, i.e., diversity stimulates economic growth. Audretsch and Keilbach (2004) suggest that regional policies focusing on the enhancement of entrepreneurial capital may prove to be more successful than other policy approaches.

Bradley (2002) asserts that states like Ireland do have some scope to influence the economic environment within which enterprises operate, whereas regions are largely 'policy takers'. Initiatives aimed at reducing bureaucracy, regulation and taxes benefit all firms and are considered effective in raising aggregate income levels in the economy. Targeted initiatives to stimulate new firm formation and growth in disadvantaged areas are usually delivered through regional and local level bodies (Armstrong and Taylor, 2000).

Ireland's County Enterprise Boards, which provide financial and management development supports to micro-enterprises, and the indigenous industry supports provided by agencies such as Enterprise Ireland, Shannon Development and Údarás na Gaeltachta are increasingly focused on enhancing the technological adaptation and export potential of Irish-owned enterprises, as recommended in the report of the Enterprise Strategy Group (2004). This is considered further in Chapter 4.

Both the flexible proactive approach required to support small-scale enterprises and the research and innovation capabilities needed to support high-technology-based firms are ameliorated by a supportive regional milieu, although, following Bradley (2002), the scope to mould the economic environment in which enterprises operate at regional level is somewhat restricted in Ireland.

Research and technological diffusion

It is generally assumed that the accumulation of knowledge (research, innovation, knowledge dissemination and human capital) and its diffusion through innovation fuel economic growth and shape economic efficiency (Armstrong and Taylor 2000; Martin, 2003). Paci and Pigliaru (1999) attribute both the long-run growth rate of leading regional economies and the technological catch-up of follower economies to their respective propensities to innovate. There is therefore a strong rationale for public investment in research and for providing a supportive environment for innovation.

O'Hara (2002: 114) describes technology and knowledge as the 'dominant motifs of the future'. Innovation is defined by the European Commission (CEC, 2004b: 5) as 'the commercial application of existing knowledge in a new context' and is viewed as resulting from the interaction of new knowledge and entrepreneurship. The understanding of innovation has evolved from its being viewed in a linear fashion to being viewed as systemic, arising primarily from the quality of interactions among all the relevant actors in the innovation process (Pike et al., 2006). Promotion of innovation includes new forms of organisation management; creativity and innovative design; new modes of service delivery; exploitation of intellectual property opportunities; and the introduction of new production methods (CEC, 2004b).

The impact of innovation on a region is contingent on the intensity of R&D activity, the potential for technological exploitation from elsewhere (technological gap), and several complementary factors. These complementary factors may be either conducive to technology diffusion, e.g. stock of physical infrastructure, critical mass and density of population, or detrimental, e.g. dominance of traditional sectors or a high unemployment rate (Cappelen et al., 2001).

One of the challenges of promoting innovation policy is that absorption or adoption capacity is generally weakest in disadvantaged regions, where the needs are greatest. Underperforming regions display lower rates of R&D investment and slower application of new technologies than innovation leaders, usually based in large diversified cities or in spatially concentrated clusters. Such regions face formidable obstacles in creating the conditions for the establishment of internationally competitive and flexibly specialised industrial clusters (Armstrong and Taylor, 2000). Contradictions are also inherent in public science policies that invest to concentrate research specialisations in a small number of locations and sectors, thus depriving disadvantaged regions of science investment (Adams et al., 2003).

At an EU level, a high degree of concentration of R&D activities is evident, with 15% of EU regions accounting for 50% of all R&D expenditure and just 4% of regions containing the leading research universities (CEC, 2004a: 51). This is even more pronounced in the concentration of R&D personnel and also in patenting activity (OECD, 2005).

An effective regional innovation system facilitates the identification of the resources available, ready access to all sources of innovation services, and successful exchanges of competences between different actors (CEC, 2006c). Innovating regions are characterised by dense networks of firms with the competences and dynamic capabilities to adopt and adapt technologies, networks[5] of untraded interdependencies and institutional 'thickness'. Innovative milieux such as at Cambridge display close networking relationships, free movement between institutions of specialised labour and high rates of new spin-off firms, thus generating wave after wave of product and process innovation (Armstrong and Taylor, 2000; CEC, 2006c). The Nordic innovation systems have adopted a 'triple helix' model whereby public science policy, institutional research and industrial innovation operate with a high degree of synchronisation. The public sector

5 The network, according to Collins (2002: 4), 'has assumed certain mythical qualities that tend to go unquestioned and at the same time can be incorporated into generalised definitions, which have considerable political value'.

acts as facilitator/animator and part-funder. Inward investment can also stimulate competitiveness by importing innovation and technology. Information and communication technologies (ICT) also play an important role in the innovation system by reducing the complexity and cost of transmitting and acquiring information (CEC, 2006d; Santinha et al., 2006).

Science and innovation policy in Ireland and in many other EU states (UK, Greece, The Netherlands) is highly centralised, with a minimal spatial dimension. This creates a tension between the pursuit of excellence and regional cohesion, thus contributing to a reinforcement of pre-existing regional disparities (Heraud and Koschatzky, 2006). At the same time, regional policymakers have an imperative to exploit regional technological and innovation assets to deliver economic gains (Perry, 2006). Perhaps a solution to this tension, as suggested by Perry, is to support selective investments in key regional locations in order to achieve a more balanced spatial distribution of clusters of research excellence, i.e., balanced excellence. Furthermore, innovation strategies that promote applied research and technology transfer and the customisation and adaptation of technologies developed elsewhere are likely to be more appropriate to weaker regions. The challenge for regional policymakers in the domain of science, technology and innovation policy in many respects mirrors the core challenge of regional and national planning, i.e. how to reconcile the potentially contradictory objectives of territorial cohesion and competitiveness.

Fiscal instruments and infrastructure investment

The pattern of public expenditure is a potent policy instrument that governments can use to address regional economic disparities, and there is considerable scope to alter government taxation and expenditure patterns to discriminate in favour of disadvantaged regions (Armstrong and Taylor, 2000). Elements of fiscal policy, i.e. taxes, transfer payments and targeted public investment, can be used as both stabilising and discretionary instruments. Progressive taxes and transfer payments, such as employment benefit, raise demand in disadvantaged regions and lower demand in prosperous regions.

The provision of targeted subsidies and tax relief to stimulate entrepreneurship and inward investment can enhance the performance of lagging regions and can be justified because of their long-run positive impact on the growth rate of the region, and of the state as a whole. The EU's state aids regime recognises that within a broad objective of eliminating trade-distorting subsidies, state aid is permissible to stimulate the development of lagging regions. Urban renewal schemes were first introduced in Ireland in 1985 to stimulate investment in derelict urban areas, and in 1998 this concept was extended to a pilot rural scheme for the upper Shannon region. However, Keane and Garvey (2006) have argued that some of these schemes have been poor value for money in terms of employment-related effects and are neither the most efficient nor effective mechanism for stimulating regeneration and addressing unemployment in the designated areas.

A low stock of public infrastructure hampers the ability of regions to be more competitive, in terms of both attracting investors and encouraging indigenous growth. Efficient transport infrastructure reduces transport costs and also influences commuting patterns (Atherton and Johnston, 2005). Investment in infrastructure endogenously promotes growth by reducing the cost of production and enabling a more efficient production environment to develop, and also attracts inward investment (Fitzgerald et al., 1999). Appropriate and strategic infrastructure development is therefore essential to enable economic growth in underdeveloped regions and will ultimately increase the attractiveness of such regions as places in which to invest, live and work.

A review of studies on the impact of investment in infrastructure on regional productivity, however, yields ambiguous results (Rosik, 2006; Dall'erba and Le Gallo, 2003). Dall'erba and Le Gallo (2003: 7) state that investments in transport infrastructure that is increasingly composed of hub-and-spoke interconnections 'do not systematically benefit the region where they are implemented', and that such networks can exacerbate disparities between regions. This point is apposite to the current investment programme by the National Roads Authority.

Martin (2000: 15) outlines how investment in infrastructure can have positive short-term effects on demand for labour and local inputs, but potentially negative long-term supply effects as reduced transaction costs may induce firms to relocate to richer regions, i.e. may induce leakage as well as linkage. Similarly, Rosik (2006) finds that richer regions benefit proportionately better from improved inter-regional transport networks, and that such investment may in fact widen disparities while providing overall efficiency gains.

Investment in telecommunications infrastructure contributes to economic efficiency, by reducing distance and time constraints, and to equity if made available to all on an equal basis (Santinha et al., 2006). However, Santinha et al. suggest that, in the absence of differential spatial policies to stimulate both the supply and demand for telecommunications infrastructure and services, a 'digital divide' and wider regional socioeconomic disparities will result. The EU Commission (CEC, 2004b: 84) acknowledges the role of ICT in fostering cohesion and balanced territorial development, but suggests that ICT policies should not be 'territorially homogenous' and should favour less developed areas. ICT was foreseen in the 1990s as a key element of regional competitive advantage and as a panacea for unbalanced regional development, but a two-tier information society has arisen from excessive concentration and centralisation (Collins, 2002). This is generally referred to as the 'digital divide', whereby disparities exist between social groups, businesses and areas in terms of their respective opportunities to access ICT (CEC, 2006d). Citing the Irish experience, Collins (2002: 16) states that ICT development 'is neither aspatial, areal, nor uniform', reflecting what he terms 'a stubborn geography underlying economic development in the information age, and not the predicted transcendence of space and distance'. Walsh (2005) identifies the need for the 'aspatiality' of telecommunications regulatory policy to be amended, so that regulatory instruments could better align with spatial development objectives.

The case for infrastructure investment is therefore quite strong from a macroeconomic efficiency perspective but is equivocal in relation to addressing regional disparities. It would also appear that the differential spatial–economic impacts of investment in national transport and telecommunications networks are not taken fully into account. This is an issue that is taken up in the review of sectoral policies in Chapter 4. Infrastructure investment may be construed as an instrument of aggregate economic efficiency, but cannot always be considered as a sufficient instrument, on its own, to reduce inter-regional disparities.

Human capital

The endogenous growth theory attributes an important role to the enhancement of human capital in promoting regional economic development. The quality of human capital is positively correlated with employability, productivity and competitiveness. It is also recognised as an important factor in raising innovation absorption capacity, the adaptation of new technologies and in the attraction of FDI. Human capital increases cumulatively on the back of existing human capital and is considered a prerequisite, in combination with other factors, to economic growth and development (López-Bazo and Moreno, 2007; OECD, 2005; Fitzgerald et al., 1999).

In a study of the 17 autonomous Spanish regions, López-Bazo and Moreno (2007) found a positive correlation between educational attainment and both private (salary) returns and aggregate social returns, in terms of productivity. They also found that the social returns were particularly strong in regions with weak relative endowments, providing a strong rationale for investment in human capital to stimulate productivity growth. The OECD (2005) describes the relationship between educational attainment and economic performance in underdeveloped regions as a complex one, citing the low availability of employment opportunities and the phenomenon of out-migration as important factors to be considered in this regard. The OECD (2005) recommends complementary policies to increase employment opportunities and the skill content of jobs. This is echoed in a study of skills demand at regional level for key specified enterprise sectors, by the Irish Expert Group on Future Skills Needs (EGFSN, 2006), which observes that where a region has a 'low-skill' equilibrium, both supply- and demand-side measures are required to address this.

The role of higher education institutions (HEIs) as knowledge producers and as institutional actors within regional innovation networks is widely acknowledged. The EGFSN (2006: 46) describes HEIs as 'potentially a central element in the portfolio of assets that contribute to a region's competitive advantage and enterprising capability'. The need for explicit regional policies in higher education in terms of lifelong learning, technology transfer, accumulation of human capital and the role of HEIs as loci for spatial clustering and as contributors to community and cultural vitality are emphasised by Thanki (1999). This role is determined by the extent and nature of their regional engagement and the type of region, whether core or peripheral (Boucher et al., 2003).

In an Irish context, it is noteworthy that four of the seven universities are located in the Greater Dublin Area, while the distribution of the institutes of technology is more spatially balanced, coinciding in particular with the designated gateway centres. The degree of educational attainment follows a distinct regional pattern, with rates generally higher in more urbanised regions and lower in rural areas, reflecting some differentials in higher education participation rates and, more significantly, high levels of intellectual out-migration. The literature briefly reviewed above suggests that investment in human capital, and in particular higher education, is a potent instrument for regional economic growth, when combined with complementary policies.

Territorial governance: Devolution

One of the central concerns of economic planning and public administration should be the determination of the appropriate territorial level for the identification and resolution of regional economic problems (Parr, 2001). Effective territorial governance is a prerequisite for progress towards territorial cohesion, defined by the European Spatial Planning Observatory Network (ESPON, 2006: 60) as 'governance in policy arenas that have a strong territorial focus, like spatial planning or regional policy'. Territorial governance is not confined to regional-level public institutions but encompasses multiple tiers, e.g. supranational (EU), national and local policy actors, and informal policymaking fora. Governance of regional policy at national level is considered separately in the next subsection. Improved territorial governance, operating through mechanisms of horizontal and vertical co-ordination, can create the conditions that enable territorial competitiveness potential to be fulfilled (Governa and Santangelo, 2006).

Many states in the EU have made moves towards some form of decentralisation, ranging from advanced forms of federalism to less extensive forms of regionalisation (McGowan and Murphy, 2003). A number of drivers have brought this about, including bottom-up regionalism, whereby regions have sought a greater degree of autonomy (e.g. in Spain and Belgium, and to a lesser extent Wales and Scotland); the transfer of functions to meso-tiers (e.g. in Sweden and France); and EU regional policies that have given rise to new regional tiers, e.g. in Ireland (Armstrong and Taylor, 2000). Summarising these processes, Hooghe and Marks (2001: 89) state that regionalism has evolved from being 'primarily a domestic phenomenon, motivated by cultural differences and discontent with national policies' to the current time in which the sources of regionalism 'lie as much outside the national state as within'.

Hutchcroft (2001) draws a distinction between devolution, de-concentration and delegation as the principal types of administrative decentralisation. He describes devolution as the handing over of power (and resources) from central government to a constituent part, a process of democratic decentralisation. De-concentration involves 'an intra-organisational transfer of particular functions and workloads from the central government to its regional or local offices', with the centre retaining the major level of authority over the content of policies (Hutchcroft 2001: 30). Delegation is described as the transfer of tasks from central government to state-owned enterprises, regional development bodies or private non-governmental firms. Advocating decentralised approaches, Jones et al. (2005: 398) state that they are:

> considered better able to address the continuing problems caused by entrenched territorial inequalities in growth, income and employment … and an enhanced, democratized, political settlement.

Porter (2003: 550) suggests that 'many of the essential determinants of economic performance are to be found at regional level' and that while national policies are essential, they are not sufficiently attuned to regional needs. The benefits that can derive from the devolution of allocative decisions include more effective matching of public service provision to geographic needs; the potential for policy innovations; and enhanced accountability for revenues raised and public service provision (Rodrígues-Pose and Gill, 2005). Morgenroth (2000) acknowledges that there are arguments in favour of introducing policies of decentralisation of public administration to subnational levels, on both administrative efficiency and subsidiarity grounds.

While it is widely claimed that the extensive involvement of regional actors is a prerequisite for successful economic development (Keating, 1997), the extent to which devolved authorities on their own can address the underlying factors that cause regional disparities is an open question. Writing from a UK devolution perspective, Adams et al. (2003: 94) state that 'the case for regional devolution appears to be strongest on democratic and public service delivery grounds'.

Rodrígues-Pose and Gill (2005) observe that it is more effective economic governance that generates economic advantages for regions, and not devolution *per se*. Morgan (2002: 797) challenges the 'unreflected assumption' that there is necessarily an economic dividend to be gained, or indeed an economic imperative, for political devolution. Morgan asserts that the relationship between devolution and economic development is ambiguous and, given that many of the economic signals are global, regions acting alone are not necessarily well placed to respond adequately. The outcomes of devolution may in fact be negative in terms of economic efficiency, equity and increased institutional costs (Jones et al., 2005; Rodrígues-Pose and Gill 2005). Inefficiencies may arise due to soft budgetary constraints and agency problems due to the separation of the governmental units that raise revenue and those that spend it. Inequities can arise due to the unequal bargaining power of regional units such that weaker, subnational areas cannot compete as effectively, thus weakening their economic base still further (Rodrígues-Pose and Gill, 2005).

Rhodes (1996) describes the evolution of the term 'governance' from implying the steering (meaning norm-setting and policy-co-ordinating) role of the state to a conception of governance as self-organising, inter-organisational networks in which the state no longer exerts a superordinate will through hierarchical chains of command. According to Rhodes's conception of governance, the state no longer holds a privileged leadership position and it may only indirectly or imperfectly steer or manage the multiplicity[6] of inter-organisational networks (comprising central and local authorities, private, regulatory, NGO and voluntary interests) now in place. Translating Rhodes's perspective to the regional level suggests that the devolution of administrative authority *per se* would not necessarily deliver more effective regional governance; rather, what matters is the capacity of

6 Morgan (2002: 804) refers to the 'bewildering array of unelected public bodies which have little local accountability' as 'quangoland' (a quango being a quasi-autonomous non-governmental organisation).

regional level authorities to actively partake in, manage and steer inter-organisational networks at multiple levels. The stimulation of endogenous potential entails the enhancement of strategic planning and horizontal co-ordination capacity at regional level as well as the creation of multilateral networks and partnerships among and between economic actors and institutions, transcending the formal institutional boundaries (Ansell, 2000). In this author's opinion, such an increase in strategic planning and co-ordination capacity presupposes a corresponding increase in strategic autonomy and access to resources, thus necessitating devolution of some additional authority to the region level.

The existence of empowered regional institutions can therefore enhance regional economic planning and development, but is not a panacea for eliminating regional disparities. In an Irish context, the potential for decentralised governance to enable Irish cities to develop differentiated policies is highlighted by O'Leary (2007). The establishment of stronger regional institutions can also strengthen institutional capacity; can make an important contribution to democratic engagement, to the provision of political leadership and consensus building, and to accountability and efficiency; and can provide channels to EU institutions, but the evidence does not point unequivocally to a rebalancing economic dividend.

'Regionalising' central government

Much of the emphasis in the regional studies literature relating to regional governance is on the region-level dimension, with insufficient emphasis on the potential for central government policies to have an enhanced territorial dimension. Parr (2001) recognises that while regional economic concerns ordinarily take second place to the macroeconomic concerns of central government, there is some scope for tailoring national policies in order to attain the desired regional outcomes. In a later paper, Parr (2005a: 127) asserts that 'there are, after all, few instances where non-spatial decision making does not have strong spatial implications'. Similarly, Commins (2006: 3) states that there is a tendency to view all of the problems *in* peripheral regions to be *of* the peripheral regions and not to recognise that these problems arise from broader underlying economic and social processes, many of which can be controlled by central governments. The question of regional economic disparities is not just a question for the underdeveloped regions themselves, but is also an issue for central government, which has a diminishing capacity to respond (Morgan, 2002; Rodrígues-Pose and Gill, 2005).

There is a dilemma at the heart of regional policy: policies that stimulate economic growth do not necessarily reduce disparities. In market liberalised economies, where state 'interference' is generally unwelcome, an important role is still assigned to central governments as strategic organisers, regulators and co-ordinators (Bradley, 2002; Jones et al., 2005). In a related vein, Laffan (2004: 14) states that the 'key domestic drivers of EU cohesion policy are the domestic core executives' rather than subnational actors.

Regionalising central government involves introducing elements of regional differentiation into central government expenditure plans, i.e. targeting investment in lagging regions, recognising the regional implications of policies introduced by all departments, avoiding spatially blind national strategies, and ensuring that the distribution of public investment does not exacerbate disparities. It includes having mechanisms in place to identify region-specific needs and priorities, and also consulting with regional agencies and institutions, in setting expenditure plans (Adams et al., 2003).

Morgenroth (2000) argues that stabilisation policies to address asymmetric regional shocks, e.g. rises in regional unemployment, as well as redistribution policies are best carried out at central government level, although there is a role for subnational government in terms of targeting areas. A further dimension of central government's role is in the administration of progressive taxation and welfare systems that indirectly serve to benefit poorer regions. The location of government offices and the procurement of government services in poorer regions is also within the gift of central government. A further role for central government identified by Parr (2001: 18) is the setting of 'consistent and attainable goals' for regional policy. Parr highlights the problem of goal evasion in regional economic planning, with policymakers opting for broad emphases or directions rather than attainable goals. This is pertinent to a consideration of Irish regional policy and is one of the issues addressed in the semi-structured interviews in Chapter 5.

Arising from the previous subsection, it could also be argued that without some degree of empowerment of region-level institutions and prioritisation/democratic preference formation at regional level, central government would not be responsive and accountable to local/regional concerns. Effective regional policy, according to Morgan (2002: 803), needs top-down initiatives 'to mobilize resources from central government and create enabling conditions' complemented by bottom-up initiatives. There is therefore a strong case for some region-level planning and prioritisation within a supportive national institutional framework, in order to achieve some degree of region-level integration of functionally differentiated government policies.

Regional development agencies

Regional development agencies (RDAs) represent a specific form of regionalised economic governance. RDAs are defined by Callinan (2000: 3) as:

> organisations concerned with economic development at the local or regional level, providing the middle ground between public authorities in charge of the collective interest and the private sector whose initiative rests on individual interest.

RDAs are geographically focused, multifunctional and semi-autonomous from central government (Ansell, 2000). Typically, RDAs conceive and deliver integrated multisectoral strategies and have the capacity to be flexible and responsive to local needs and to engage in collaborative multi-partner alliances. RDAs can, according to Danson (2003), reduce localised market failures, such as imperfect information and risk aversion and so-called 'government failure', due to their localised market orientation. RDAs can achieve synergies through the integration of multiple interventions, often combining regional, sectoral and human capital policies and, by being at a remove from central and local government, they can take a long-term strategic perspective. RDAs also offer the advantage of building direct trust-based relationships with the private sector.

Although RDAs, as part of the quango sector, are open to charges of weak democratic accountability, they have been the preferred vehicle to deliver regional economic development strategies in several (mostly large) EU countries (Danson, 2003). Two examples of RDAs in Ireland are Shannon Development and Udarás na Gaeltachta. In 2005, the Minister for Enterprise, Trade and Employment proposed that the enterprise support functions of Shannon Development should be assumed by Enterprise Ireland and IDA Ireland (Department of Enterprise, Trade and Employment, 2005). The agencies responsible for enterprise development are primarily national agencies, with their regional offices having some delegated functions; they are not formally accountable to regional political institutions.

Spatial planning

Spatial planning is increasingly being deployed as an instrument of regional policy. The underlying rationale for the European Spatial Development Perspective (ESDP) and the Irish National Spatial Strategy (NSS) is that improved spatial structuring is a prerequisite for balanced regional development. Spatial planning has evolved from a focus on land use planning to encompass the reinforcement of cohesion, and a concern with correcting 'regional asymmetries … and ensuring conditions favorable to the development of economic, social and cultural activities' (Santinha et al., 2006: 9).

Polycentric development, involving the creation of new growth centres outside the core areas, has been described by Faludi (2006: 669) as the 'contemporary paradigm of regional development'. This concept, as described earlier, implies that competitive advantage, regionally balanced development and a lessening of economic and demographic concentration, can all be gained from the creation of several globally integrated economic zones (Faludi, 2006).

In a study commissioned by the Department of the Environment, Heritage and Local Government and Forfás, Fitzpatrick Associates et al. (2006) cite the international and national evidence in support of strategically targeting and prioritising investment in major urban centres as the basis for successful regional economic development. The study emphasises the need for a renewed commitment to investment prioritisation and improved co-ordination across the key public and private stakeholders in order for the designated gateways to be effective in stimulating regional development.

Spatial planning in the form of multiple growth centre strategies is concerned with achieving the balanced development of strategic urban centres that possess the physical, social and cultural attributes that enable them to be competitive internationally, and to drive the economic development of their hinterlands. Thus, spatial planning has both inward- and outward-oriented objectives (Fitzpatrick Associates et al., 2006). The NSS is considered in detail in Chapter 4.

Policy coherence and policy effectiveness

The previous sections in this chapter have reviewed the literature on the drivers and measurement of regional economic growth and the rationale, evolution and typologies of regional policy. In order to address the central question of the coherence of Irish regional policy, this section reviews the concepts of policy coherence and policy effectiveness and proposes a new framework for assessing policy coherence.

Recent governance and public policy literature places considerable emphasis on the shift from a 'government' paradigm, i.e. the application of authority to accomplish societal goals, to a 'governance' paradigm, the 'pluralisation' of policy actors and the creation of 'horizontalist' interdependences between state and non-state actors in determining and delivering public policy objectives (Di Francesco, 2001; Hill & Hupe, 2002). This views policymaking as a complex interplay between pluri-centric, interdependent actors across institutional boundaries, to achieve public policy goals, recognising the political–social contexts and the multiple loci and layers that effect policy formulation and implementation (Hill & Hupe, 2002). Added to this are the 'hollowing-out' thesis and the 'marketisation' of public policy management, arising from public sector reforms, which gives rise to fragmentation and a weakening of central institutional co-ordination capacity and control (Rhodes, 1994). These developments have an impact on the ability of central government and its agencies to steer and manage public policy coherently (Di Francesco, 2001). In this context, governmental authority is no longer viewed as power exercised 'over' others through vertical chains of command, but rather as the power to accomplish collective goals; policy direction no longer comes solely from above, but arises from collaborative consensus-building processes. Process management, network building, consultative policy resolution and collaboration capacity take on added importance, although national governments retain a monopoly on legislative power and veto power over indispensable resources (Hill and Hupe, 2002).

Policy coherence is viewed as an imperative of public policy and requires both external and internal policy consistency (Forster and Stokke, 1999). Internal consistency implies a logical policy framework, with coherence between policy goals, objectives and modalities (European Union, 2006). External policy coherence is defined by the OECD (1996: 8) as 'an overall state of mutual consistency among different policies'. Effective external policy coherence requires that intended results and objectives from one particular policy domain should not be frustrated and undermined as a consequence of another policy, which can lead to policy failure and wastage of resources. The procedural nature of co-ordination is emphasised by Di Francesco (2001), who contends that policy coherence is best pursued through procedures of mutual adjustment and partisan adaptation by policymaking bodies, rather than through inflexible, interventionist control over policy outcomes.

In democratic systems with multiple and competing policy interests, absolute policy coherence, in which the objectives of one policy domain should permeate and be evident in all related policy domains, is difficult to attain. Conflicting objectives must therefore be arbitrated and re-prioritised over time (Di Francesco, 2001; Fresco, 2004; European Union, 2006). Recognising that policy outcomes are often influenced by factors outside the direct control of policymakers, Hill and Hupe (2002: 80) state that the expectation that policymakers will always have clear objectives based on valid causal theories is unrealistic. Nevertheless, clear congruent objectives, explicit outcomes and a rationally based policy design are desirable, if not always achievable.

The European Union (2006: 17–18), in a scoping paper on policy coherence in to the EU's external aid programmes to developing countries, identifies three overarching mechanisms that can be expected to promote policy coherence:

1. a strong political commitment, with clear policy objectives and explicit investment criteria
2. adequate institutional architecture, inter-sectoral co-ordination and mechanisms for dialogue with all relevant agents
3. strategic policy analysis capacity to support evidence-based policymaking.

Fresco (2004) suggests that policy coherence should be approached both horizontally and vertically. Horizontal coherence requires engagement across governmental bodies, agencies and non-governmental actors. Vertical coherence operates within a multilevel governance framework reflecting supranational institutional goals and subnational policy competences.

Figure 2.2: A policy coherence framework

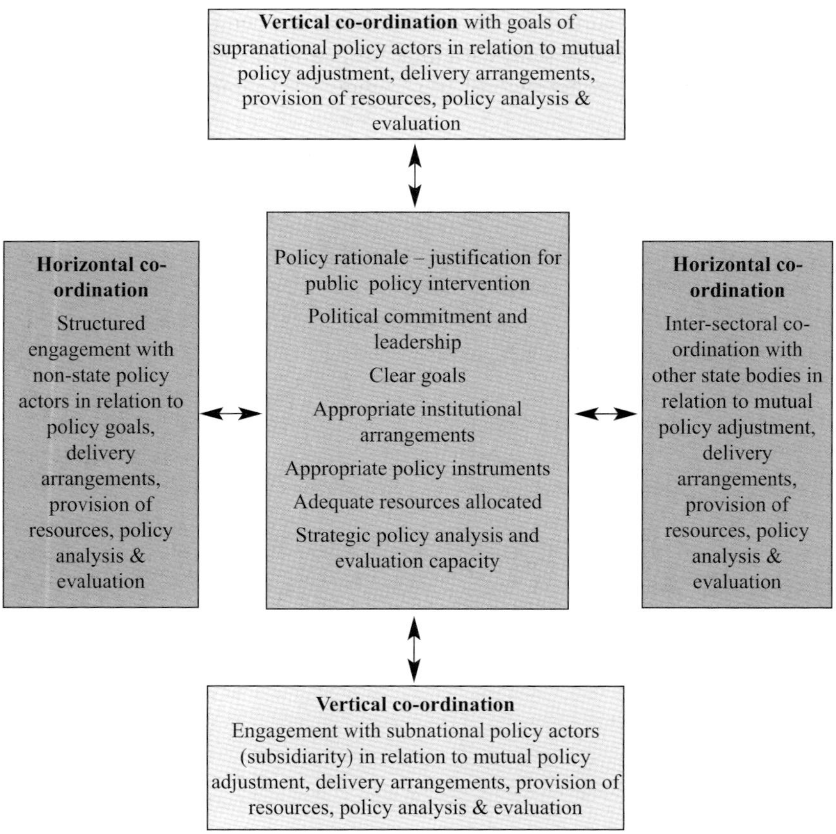

The framework shown in Figure 2.2 has been developed, based on the above literature, to represent the elements of a coherent policy framework, including internal and external elements and the connections between them. The framework assumes that the policy domain is primarily a central government competence and recognises the vertical and horizontal linkages that may apply. Its internal elements represent the coherence of the logical arrangements in place for effective policy development, delivery and review. It recognises that there should be a clear rationale for public policy intervention and political commitment and leadership to effect the desired policy response.

In a regional policy context, strong regional and local leadership can promote dynamism and self-reliance (O'Hara et al., 2008). Changes in political priorities may effect changes in the scope, goals, resource allocations or institutional arrangements of the policy framework. The framework also assumes that the goals of the policy are clear and measurable and that appropriate institutional arrangements and adequate resources are applied to manage the policy effectively, consistent with the policy goals. Hill and Hupe (2002: 145) describe situations where there is 'no realistic consideration of the relationship between means and ends' as 'symbolic policy'. Consistent with the European Union's criteria, as set out above, the internal coherence of the framework requires strategic policy analysis capacity to be in place to support evidence-based policy, identify trends and drivers that are relevant to the policy, and evaluate policy delivery against goals. Some of the elements considered internal in the framework may in part reside externally, e.g. policy implementation, resource allocation and strategic policy analysis capacity.

The external elements of the framework include both horizontal and vertical co-ordination arrangements. The horizontal interdependences referred to above include processes for mutual policy adjustment with other state bodies and processes for structured dialogue with non-governmental bodies, including social movements and representative groups. This interactive form of policymaking is often termed 'co-production' and is defined by Hill and Hupe (2002: 135) as 'joint contributions delivered by partners in a system'. Through co-production, policy goals and implementation arrangements become 'pragmatised' via a process of negotiation, and implementation tasks are fulfilled within joint frameworks. The quality of horizontal inter-organisational relationships and the disposition and level of acceptance by policy implementers towards a policy mandate are considered important determinants of successful and coherent policy implementation (Hill and Hupe, 2002). The vertical dimensions include policy co-ordination with the relevant policies of supranational actors, e.g. the EU, and co-ordination with subnational (local and regional) public bodies. For example, it is acknowledged in the ESDP that while many EU policies do not have a specific spatial character, they do have significant territorial impacts and can 'unintentionally aggravate disparities in regional development' (CEC, 1999: 19).

In this framework, both the internal and external actors may be significant political influencers, may be agents for policy delivery and resource providers, and may be sources of strategic policy analysis. In this context, regional bodies have a legitimate claim to participate fully in the co-production of regional policy. Significant influence may be applied to change the systems and structures in order to influence current and future outcomes – meta-policymaking (Hill, 1997: 22). An analysis of policy coherence also includes the nature and quality of the interconnections between the internal and external actors.

Policy effectiveness is both the perceived adequacy of a policy to meet its intended goals and its success in actually doing so. Effectiveness is a useful measure of the functionality of policy actions as well as an assessment of the variance between the intended and actual outcomes of a defined policy (Hill & Hupe, 2002). Addressing the issue of effectiveness presupposes that policymakers 'have the measure' of what is required to achieve the intended outcomes of the policy, and that the desired outcomes are clear. Analysis of policy effectiveness can determine whether the policy framework is the correct one, with valid goals, and also if it is being properly operationalised, i.e. avoidance of implementation failure.

Chapter conclusions

This chapter has provided a theoretical orientation for the study by reviewing the literature on the principal economic growth theories, the influential concepts of territorial cohesion, polycentric development and competitiveness, and the measurement of regional performance. A typology of regional policy approaches – investment-related, governance-related and spatial planning – was provided, and these were reviewed.

The economic growth models, although predicting somewhat contrasting outcomes, provided the theoretical basis for the different strands of investment policies deployed by governments over recent decades. Regions do not converge in the absence of appropriate policies, and as understandings of the underlying spatial–economic mechanisms that shape the relative economic performance of regions improve, the potential to design more appropriate policy interventions is enhanced.

Notwithstanding the largely non-interventionist stance of neoliberal economic models, there are cogent economic, social and political arguments in favour of states pursuing proactive regional policies. The choice of investment strategies, the level of intervention engaged in and the distribution of authority between national and subnational authorities are ultimately determined by the interplay of national and regional economic policy objectives, as predominantly set by national government. Clear policy goals and appropriate national and region-level policy planning and implementation, including arrangements for enhanced co-operation between the authorities responsible for sectoral and spatial policies, are essential to set an appropriate framework for regional investment and spatial planning.

This chapter has provided a useful context within which to consider the strategic direction of Irish regional policy and recent socioeconomic trends – the subject of Chapter 4. Moreover, the chapter has raised several issues for further exploration in the in-depth interviews. These include the rationale for Irish regional policy, the influence of the alternative conceptual frameworks on defining the direction of regional policy, the selection of investment priorities to attain the stated goals, and the institutional framework within which to design and deliver these policies.

Many of the core dilemmas facing regional policymakers have been touched on in this chapter. These include: reconciling cohesion (equity) and competitiveness (efficiency) goals; anticipating and counteracting the spatial concentration of economic activity (altering economic geography); addressing the challenges posed in weaker regions of pursuing polycentric, inward investment and regional innovation strategies; choosing between spatial and people-centred approaches; and overcoming the differential spatial impacts of R&D, ICT and transport investment strategies. Linked with the cohesion–competitiveness dilemma is the distinction between regional development policies that seek to promote development in all regions and policies that seek to narrow disparities between regions. FDI is likely to be less significant in the future; policies to promote indigenous enterprise development will be more important.

A framework within which the coherence of regional policy and its effectiveness can be determined has been developed. This emphasises the importance of internal and external consistency, the quality of interactions and policy synergies as the building blocks of public policy coherence.

3

Methodology

The proposition tested in this study is that regional policy in the Republic of Ireland lacks coherence and that a more coherent and effective regional policy is possible, with complementary spatial planning policies, sectoral investment strategies and governance arrangements. The overall aim of the study was to assess how the coherence of Irish regional policy can be improved and the implications of this for regional investment strategies, spatial planning and the governance of regional policy at central and regional levels, taking account of current influential theoretical perspectives, the politico-institutional setting and the prevailing socioeconomic context.

This chapter sets out the approach that was adopted to design and carry out the study. It commences with an outline of the philosophical stance that has influenced the methodological approach, analysis and interpretation of the data. The design of the research instruments used is described and the method of selection of questions and interviewees, with reference to the specific research objectives, is outlined. Finally, the methods used to gather, assimilate and interpret the data and to ensure the quality of the research are described.

Research philosophy

Social research is a purposive, rigorous investigation of a phenomenon with the aim of generating new knowledge or understandings (Sarantakos, 2005). It is generally recognised that the choice of a research method (or methods) must take account of some assumptions about the nature of knowledge and how it is obtained, as well as some assumptions about the nature of the subject or phenomenon being researched (Morgan and Smircich, 1980). Theoretical perspectives are the philosophical stances and assumptions that provide the basis for the chosen research methodology, because 'different ways of viewing the world shape different ways of researching the world' (Crotty, 2003: 66). The assumptions made about the nature of reality (ontological perspective) and the status that can be ascribed to the knowledge attained through research (epistemological perspective) shape the meaning of the research questions posed, the methodology chosen, the type of evidence that will be gathered and the interpretability of the research findings (Crossman, 2003; Crotty, 2003; Sarantakos, 2005). Research designs are therefore appropriate in particular contexts and depend also on the nature of the research questions posed.

The ontological perspective adopted in this research study was that while reliable objective quantified data and trends are available, people's perceptions of the reality of regional issues may differ and there can be several 'validly' held interpretations of the same phenomenon. This does not preclude such interpretations from being subject to critical appraisal, as some will be found to be more plausible, accurate and supportable truth claims than others. The implications of this for the research design were that exclusively quantitative approaches would not have been sufficient to meet the overall aims of the study and that a combination of quantitative and qualitative approaches was required. It also required that the role, values and perspective of the researcher should be made explicit.

Epistemology is concerned with the different ways of knowing, what constitutes accepted knowledge in a particular field and how it can be obtained. This study has descriptive, evaluative and normative dimensions. The knowledge attained is a reflection of the opinions, experiences, and judgements of the interviewees, interpreted by the researcher and correlated with statistical and documentary evidence. This study was broadly interpretivist in epistemological orientation, with its focus on how selected interviewees viewed Irish regional policy, but also placed some emphasis on the objectivity of the primary and secondary data regarding current national and selected sectoral strategies and regional socioeconomic trends, and on the objective nature of external (e.g. EU) policy drivers.

Concepts such as 'regional competitiveness' and 'territorial cohesion' permeate this study. It is acknowledged that several plausible representations or nuanced understandings of these concepts may exist, influenced by prevailing paradigms. The understandings of these concepts held by key influencers are one factor that orients public policy related to regional policy in Ireland. Bryman (2004: 271) refers to concepts as 'sensitising' rather than definitive, providing no more than a sense of reference. Drawing on Kuhn (1970), Crotty (2003) describes paradigms as the particular way an epistemic community makes sense of the world, representing a settled consensus and establishing the parameters of research.

Research strategy

Quantitative and qualitative approaches represent two broad research strategies. Quantitative research is concerned with measurement and is usually committed to a positivist epistemology. Qualitative research, on the other hand, is descriptive, concerned with explanation rather than measurement, and is post-positivist. However, research strategies do not necessarily conform fully with these characteristics, and (as is the case with this study) quantitative and qualitative research methods can be used in conjunction with each other, often as a means of triangulating and adding validity to the findings (Crossman, 2003).

Although much analysis of regional socioeconomic drivers and trends is based on the rich foundations of statistically valid quantified data and trends, Crang (2002: 648) notes that economic geography has begun to pay increasing attention to qualitative methods to inform understandings. This amounts to studies analysing generalised global processes through the more localised social milieu where economic processes can be observed. Hill and Hupe (2002) stress the complexity of effective public policy design and privilege qualitative studies of factors that affect implementation over evaluative studies of goal attainment. Bryman (2004: 280) emphasises the added value of qualitative approaches, including the adoption of an empathetic approach, 'privileging the subjective views' of respondents, the value of rich contextual description with a premium on detailed descriptions of social settings, and the possibility of capturing how events unfold and processes operate over time. Bryman (2004: 285) notes that the findings of qualitative research are context-specific and are intended to generalise to theory, not to populations, with the 'cogency' of the theoretical inferences being more important than absolute generalisability.

In this study a combination of quantitative and qualitative approaches was used. This enabled flexibility in the use of research instruments – the incorporation of analysis of primary and secondary data sources along with analysis of the outcomes of the semi-structured interviews – to inform the conclusions of the study. This approach maximises the added value of the research study and enables a degree of triangulation of the findings, lending them greater validity.

Research methods

The research methods chosen for this study comprised the following elements:

1. qualitative content analysis of national investment plans and selected sectoral strategies
2. analysis of key regional socioeconomic trends, based on quantified statistical data
3. semi-structured interviews with leading personnel.

Qualitative content analysis

Primary source documents provide first-hand unmediated evidence on a topic under study. Qualitative content analysis of primary documents 'comprises searching out of underlying themes in the materials being analysed' (Bryman, 2004: 392). Official government documents provide a primary source of evidence of the activities, functions and policies of government bodies. Content analysis is considered by Bryman (2004) to be a transparent, replicable, unobtrusive research method with the opportunity for longitudinal analysis. Sarantakos (2005) highlights the retrospectivity and convenience of qualitative content analysis of authentic publications. The main disadvantage of this method, according to Bryman (2004: 197) is the risk of 'non-correspondence of interpretation' between the document author(s) and the researcher.

In this study, the published national investment and spatial plans and selected sectoral strategies, as set out by government, were recognised as an important primary source, reflecting the official policy and plans of government. These were reviewed with an emphasis on the overall strategic approach proposed and the explicit regional development content. In addition, some secondary analysis in the form of published critiques of these policy documents was reviewed and incorporated into the analysis. This provided a valuable complement to the outcomes of the semi-structured interviews and the statistical information presented in Chapter 4.

The sectoral strategies analysed were restricted to four specific areas – transport infrastructure; science and innovation; indigenous enterprise development; and foreign direct investment – as these were considered most relevant to regional investment strategies.

Analysis of regional socioeconomic trends

Secondary analysis of officially published statistics provides an accessible, reliable source of data with the potential for multi-annual comparative analysis. For example, the official statistics published by the Central Statistics Office (CSO) provide a valuable source of secondary information on regional socioeconomic trends: readily available quantitative data that have been collected consistently over many years.

One of the disadvantages of using data that may have been published for other purposes is that the range of variables or the spatial scale to which the data apply may not be consistent with the specific scope of the researcher's study (Bryman, 2004). There are also definitional issues that have to be taken into account such that official crime or joblessness data, for instance, may not reflect the complete picture or accord with the definition being applied by a researcher.

In terms of regional data, the 'County Incomes and Regional GDP' series, which is published annually (but with a two-year time lag) provides data on regional GVA and county and regional disposable incomes, which can be used to establish trends in the relative performance of regions on two of the most commonly used indicators. In addition, some analyses that have been conducted on the sources of regional disparities in Ireland were reviewed. This is relevant to the consideration of the scale and trends of regional disparities in Ireland and provides a useful reference point for the qualitative analysis that arises from the semi-structured interviews. As there are potentially dozens of alternative socioeconomic indicators that could be used to assess relative regional performance over a defined time period, a representative sample of six indicators was chosen, reflecting trends in population, economic output, disposable incomes, labour force, sectoral structure and innovation activity.

Semi-structured interviews

Welch et al. (1999: 14) define the challenge of the interview situation as being the creation of 'space for intellectual discussion and reflection' in order to elicit views of the interviewees on the research topic. Three broad categories of interview are used in research. Unstructured interviews are described by Leech (2002) as 'conversations' that can provide insight, but are not useful for testing hypotheses. Structured interviews deploy predetermined sets of questions in which the possible categories of response are already known, and are commonly used in quantitative research methodologies. The third type, semi-structured interviews, was chosen for this study because the use of open-ended questions provided detail and depth and a means to elicit the respondents' perspectives. In semi-structured interviews the question schedule does not have to be followed rigidly and interviewees have wide scope in how to respond. Supplementary questions can be asked. As recommended by Bryman (2004), an interview guide was prepared in order to provide some focus to the interview, allowing potentially fruitful alternative lines of enquiry to emerge during the interview process.

The semi-structured interviews were undertaken with leading personnel in national and regional organisations and academic institutions and representatives of social partner organisations, who have policy responsibility for, or an influence on, regional policy in Ireland. These are among what could be termed the 'key influencers' of Irish regional policy. The bias towards leading personnel is justified on the basis that the research is not intended as a 'snapshot' of public opinion on regional policy issues but as a purposive discursive exercise with key policy influencers in order to determine their perspective on current regional policy issues.

Many of the challenges of interviewing 'elites' as described by Welch et al. (1999) could also apply to interviewing key policy influencers. These challenges include maintaining academic integrity while at the same time 'balancing the power of the influential elite'; negotiating access to selected interviewees; and recognising cultural and 'status' gaps between the interviewer and interviewee (Welch et al., 1999: 5). Much of the emphasis in qualitative research literature is on interviewing non-elites, e.g. socially marginalised groups, where the balance of power favours the interviewer. The interviewer in elite interviews, on the other hand, may be expected to justify the relevance, potential benefits and non-threatening nature of the research to the interviewee, as well as their own credentials and institutional sponsorship in order to obtain consent. As a 'supplicant', the researcher may feel obliged to refrain from posing challenging research questions.

Nevertheless, the strength of qualitative studies collecting data from in-depth interviews, according to Welch et al. (1999: 2), is the opportunity to examine 'dynamic, context-dependent and interactive phenomena'. They also note that elites may be more accustomed to engaging in complex conceptual discourse, but may dominate the discussion and seek to 'win over' the researcher to their point of view. A further potential risk is that elite interviewees in defending their own or their organisation's policies may not be fully open to the interviewer and may resort to quoting the 'party line'.

Welch et al. (1999) warn against considering elite interviews as superior to non-elite interviews in conferring credibility or authority on the findings. A further potential weakness identified by Crang (2002) is a failure to recognise that elite interviewees do not necessarily have perfect knowledge of a situation.

Design of research instrument and selection of interviewees

This section focuses on the design of the semi-structured questionnaire, the selection of interviewees and the organisation of the interviews.

Semi-structured interview guide

As suggested by Bryman (2004), the interview guide was constructed in order to elicit responses to the central research questions posed, and a preferred question order was determined, which was subject to change during the interviews. Each theme in the interview guide derives from one or more of the following:

1. the research questions posed and the particular focus of the study
2. key issues and concepts that arose from the literature review
3. the elements of the policy coherence framework devised for this study.

A total of 10 thematic areas were identified. The rationale for inclusion of each theme is set out in Table 3.1.

It was considered unnecessary to pilot the interview guide, as would be the case for structured interviews, as the flexible semi-structured format allowed questions to be rephrased or supplementary questions to be asked within the themes of the interview guide.

Table 3.1: Rationale for selection of research themes

Theme	Purpose
1. *Rationale* Do you think that Ireland should have a regional policy and what should the main elements of that policy be?	To establish what the rationale for regional policy in Ireland is and what the elements of the policy should be. All public policies should have an explicit rationale and this could be correlated with the range of potential rationales discussed in the literature review.
2. *Goal of current regional policy* What do you consider to be the principal features of Irish regional policy and what would you consider its goals to be?	To determine what the interviewees consider the principal instruments and the policy goals in Irish regional policy to be. Goal definition is an important element in policy planning and analysis and the features of the policy instruments used to achieve the goal can be reviewed in the context of the typology set out in the literature review.
3. *Evaluate regional policy* How effective do you believe current regional policy is?	To assess the effectiveness of regional policy in Ireland in attaining its goals from the perspective of the interviewees. This is one of the central questions of the study.
4. *Convergence/divergence forces* What forces do you consider are driving regional convergence and/or divergence in Ireland?	To identify the forces that currently, or could potentially, lead to greater economic convergence or divergence in Ireland. An understanding of these forces enables an assessment of the potential effectiveness of policies to accentuate the positive forces and mitigate the negative forces.

Theme	Purpose
5. *Overarching goal/driver* Which of these would you consider should be the predominant goal of Irish regional policy? • Cohesion – convergence in the economic performance of all regions • Competitiveness – raising productivity and employment levels, nationally and/or regionally • Polycentric development – more balanced spatial structuring	To ascertain from the interviewees which of the alternative concepts should be the predominant influencer of Irish regional policy. These influential concepts feature prominently in the contemporary literature on regional policy.
6. *Measurement criteria* By what criteria should comparative regional performance be measured and evaluated?	To establish from the interviewees the indicators that they consider should be used to assess the comparative performance of regions. This question is intended to explore the key issue of measuring comparative regional performance.
7. *Investment planning* What types of investment policies would you consider most conducive to achieving your suggested goal for regional policy?	To identify the investment strategies considered by the interviewees to be the most appropriate to attain their suggested goals for regional policy. The process of preparing strategies and the content of the strategies are among the three dimensions of regional policy that are the focus of this study.
8. *Spatial planning* How would you suggest that more effective spatial planning could be achieved in Ireland?	To elicit the views of the interviewees on effective spatial planning in Ireland, another of the dimensions of regional policy that is the focus of this study. This could be correlated with the literature on polycentric development and the review of the National Spatial Strategy.
9. *Governance arrangements* Who do you consider should be responsible for drawing up, implementing and evaluating investment plans and spatial frameworks?	To determine the views of the interviewees on the governance of regional policy in Ireland, and in particular on responsibility for drawing up, implementing and evaluating investment plans and spatial frameworks. Governance is an important dimension of regional policy.

Theme	Purpose
10. Implications for regional bodies What specific roles should be played by region-level bodies and what powers (if any) should be devolved to regional bodies?	To identify the role that should be played by regional bodies in Ireland. Devolution as a policy instrument is discussed in the literature review and its application in Ireland's politico-institutional context is considered by the interviewees.

Selection of interviewees

In light of the specialised nature of the issues to be explored in this study, and the need for some existing understanding among interviewees of the underlying concepts, interviewees were selected from a number of categories or stratified 'panels'. The reason for the stratification of interviewees was to obtain feedback from several perspectives – national, regional, academic and representative social partner organisations – such that no one perspective is over-represented. In an Irish regional policy context, the key influencers are senior officials in government departments and agencies, regional economists and geographers who undertake research and provide consultancy services to government in this field, senior executives in subnational public bodies (including one local authority manager) and senior representatives of the social partner organisations. A list of the interviewees is provided in Appendix 1.

Interviewees were selected on the basis of one or more of the following:

- current position in which they have policy responsibility in one of four selected sectoral fields: transport infrastructure, science and innovation, indigenous enterprise and foreign direct investment
- current position in which they have responsibility for co-ordination of public investment strategies, competitiveness or spatial planning
- have previously published papers or have conducted evaluations on Irish regional issues
- senior position in a social partner or related organisation that influences public policy
- senior position in a region-based organisation or in the regions division of a national body.

Organisation of interviews

The 24 interviews were conducted over an 11-month period between August 2007 and July 2008. The process involved an initial telephone contact with the prospective interviewee to introduce the research and to obtain an expression of willingness to be interviewed and, preferably, agreement on a suitable date for the interview. This was followed up immediately with a letter setting out the background aims of the study, its context within the DGov Programme,[7] the identity of the supervisor, the reason why they had been selected and the broad research questions. The introductory letter (Appendix 3) also provided a commitment regarding the observation of research ethics and confidentiality, and set out the arrangements for recording the interviews. A copy of the interview guide was attached to each letter.

In conducting semi-structured interviews, Leech (2002) emphasises the importance of gaining rapport, using active listening techniques, and the use of several question types, such as ‘grand tour questions’, prompts and example questions. Leech advocates an approach that views the researcher as professional, knowledgeable and curious. Using this qualitative interview method, complex issues can be discussed in depth and the emphasis can be adjusted during the interview. Further to this, the interviewee could play a role in defining the important issues (Kvale, 1996; Leech, 2002; Bryman, 2004). In conducting the interviews, rapport was gained by first of all introducing the objectives and format of the study and reiterating the commitment to confidentiality as per the letter of introduction, referred to above. Many of the interviewees were known professionally to the researcher and this also helped to establish rapport.

With the consent of all interviewees, the interviews were recorded – initially this was done on a hand-held digital recording device, but following equipment failure during two early interviews, the remaining interviews were recorded using recording software (Audacity) on a mobile computer. An advantage of recording interviews is that during the interview the conflicting demands on the interviewer of keeping comprehensive notes, while at the same time ‘steering’ the course of the interview and following up on fruitful lines of questioning, can be avoided. A second advantage is that following the interview a full transcript can be made.

A disadvantage of this approach is that interviewees may be more guarded in their ‘on the record’ responses. An alternative approach of documenting only the key issues and pertinent points made in response to the questions was considered, but was viewed as unsatisfactory, as the significance of some key issues might be missed. Full transcripts of the interviews were made (with the exception of the two unrecorded interviews referred to above, in which cases summary notes were made).

---

7 The Doctorate in Governance (DGov) is a four-year part-time professional doctoral programme offered jointly by the Institute of Public Administration (IPA) and Queen’s University Belfast. It comprises the study of eight modules and the preparation of a doctoral thesis founded on research undertaken by students.

Data analysis

The analysis of qualitative data has some distinct features that differentiate it from quantitative analysis. In qualitative analysis, data collection, analysis, interpretation and the construction of conditional propositions is an iterative and dynamic process. Qualitative analysis follows processes of concept refinement and confirmation, identification of patterns and the establishment of provisional generalisations that can, if verified, lead to the construction of substantive theory (Sarantakos, 2005). In qualitative data analysis, there is a 'repetitive interplay between the collection and analysis of data', and the emerging concepts influence the focus and choice of further data collection (Bryman, 2004: 399). It follows a process of conceptually organising the unstructured data collected, and the recursive collection of new data, until 'theoretical' saturation is reached, i.e. until no new relevant concepts emerge (Sarantakos, 2005).

The analysis of the transcripts of the semi-structured interviews followed the qualitative data analysis approach, as described above. This involved the initial identification and labelling of salient points, or concepts, that had potential significance. Also, the final selection of interviewees was not completed until after many of the interviews had been conducted.

These concepts were further analysed and regrouped as categories, loosely following the key research themes. The findings of the study are presented in Chapter 5 on the basis of the most significant common themes. These themes, which were most revealing and have most applicability, were triangulated with the outcome of the content analysis and trend analysis described in Chapter 4, and these influenced the conclusions of this study.

It is recognised that the qualitative data analysis approach adopted has some potential limitations. First, the salient concepts identified are usually conditioned by the existing conceptual knowledge of the researcher; second, potentially relevant concepts may be excluded from further analysis if not apparently relevant to the predetermined research questions in the interview guide (Bryman, 2003). However, the researcher's existing knowledge and specific fields of interest provided a focus to the data collection, such that theoretical saturation may be reached sooner, thus reducing the overall time and cost of the study.

Ethics, confidentiality and position of the researcher

The research approach adopted followed the ethical principles of obtaining informed consent, upholding confidentiality, and refraining from the use of coercion, the fabrication, falsification or concealment of any research findings or the plagiarisation of the work of others.

The nature of this research study did not lend itself to a value-free approach. The researcher has identified the research area, formulated the research questions, chosen the research method, designed the main research instrument, selected the interviewees, conducted the interviews, compiled and interpreted the findings, and drawn the conclusions. In addition, during the course of this study, the researcher was employed by the Border, Midland and Western (BMW) Regional Assembly, a regional body that plays an important role in the management of EU structural funds, the monitoring of public investment in the BMW region and the submission of policy papers on various issues of relevance to regional policy.

Following Fay (1996), regarding the need for the position of the researcher to be explicit, the researcher brought to this study a desire to elaborate a coherent regional policy for Ireland that is appropriate to current circumstances, and a curiosity to establish how selected interviewees viewed existing policy approaches and institutional arrangements, and what policy approaches they would consider the most effective in order to improve the coherence of Irish regional policy.

Having an 'insider status' was both advantageous and problematic. The advantages were that the researcher was knowledgeable about the subject area, had a good initial understanding of the key issues and pertinent themes, was familiar with some of the relevant literature and studies and knew professionally many of the key influencers who were interviewed over the course of the study. The main disadvantage was the risk of personal bias or preconceptions that could influence the interpretation of the findings. To avoid this, the researcher had to allow a diversity of opinions to be expressed by the 24 interviewees and also had to ensure that alternative views were captured and reported in the findings and that the conclusions ultimately drawn were reflective of the diverse views expressed throughout the study.

Ensuring the quality of the research

In order to ensure that the outcomes of this research study can be considered valid and trustworthy, the research process must meet the appropriate quality criteria. Bryman (2004) sets out five criteria for effective research methodology:

1. validity
2. reliability
3. replicability
4. generalisability
5. objectivity.

Validity is considered the most important criterion and concerns the integrity and rigour of the research process and the plausibility of the conclusions generated. Reliability is the accuracy and consistency of the method(s) used to measure or to evaluate phenomena. It is sometimes referred to as 'measurement validity' and is of particular concern in quantitative research methods (Bryman, 2004). Replicability as a criterion is the requirement that the research process be sufficiently transparent that it can be repeated or reproduced. Generalisability, often termed 'external validity', relates to the applicability of the findings beyond the immediate research group (Bryman, 2004). Objectivity is the elimination of subjective bias in research (Fay, 1996). The principle of objective truth amenable to scientific enquiry has been 'the epistemological foundation of Western science' (Crotty, 2003: 42). Following Lincoln and Guba (1985), Crang (2002) posits that credibility (plausibility), transferability (wider applicability), dependability (reliability) and confirmability (a proxy for objectivity) should be the yardsticks in qualitative research.

Given that this study had quantitative and qualitative elements, both sets of criteria can be applied. The validity or credibility of the study rests on ensuring that the conclusions are congruent with the primary data reviewed and the perspectives offered by the interviewees. The reliability or dependability of the findings is determined by their consistency with those of any similar studies. Clearly documenting the research methodology and the rationale for the approach taken, and making available the research instruments used, ensures transparency and, as highlighted by Bryman (2004), this enables the research to be replicated elsewhere.

An implication of adopting (in part) a constructivist framework is that, since understandings are constructions and are context-specific, they are not truly generalisable. Even though many of the overarching policy drivers are applicable to regions elsewhere, the particular institutional context in which this study was conducted is unique to Ireland. Nevertheless, the general principles of the multi-level co-production of sectoral and spatial strategies, appropriate territorial governance and spatial planning frameworks are broadly applicable and this study provides an insight into their application in Ireland. Ensuring that a wide array of possible perspectives was taken into account and that other sources of data (primary and secondary) were incorporated into the study aided the objectivity of the findings.

Chapter conclusions

The focus of this research study is on the coherence and effectiveness of Irish regional policy, and in particular the dimensions of that policy related to strategic investment planning, spatial planning and regional governance. The use of an exclusively quantitative or qualitative approach was considered insufficient to meet the study's overall aims. The approach taken combined an analysis of primary and secondary documentary sources and statistical trends with the outcomes of 24 recorded semi-structured interviews with leading personnel in four broad categories: government departments and national agencies; subnational public bodies; selected academic experts; and social partner bodies who are active players in the policy development, implementation and evaluation processes.

The themes of the semi-structured interviews took account of the predefined research questions, the concepts reviewed in the theoretical literature and the elements of the policy coherence framework developed in Chapter 2. The collection and analysis of the data followed an iterative process, consistent with the principles of qualitative data analysis. The salient concepts that emerged from this process were correlated with those from the content analysis of key national and selected sectoral strategies and socioeconomic trends.

4

Regional Development Policy in Ireland

The aim of this chapter is to review a range of primary and secondary documentary and statistical sources in order to gain an understanding of the features and effectiveness of Irish regional policies and their coherence with regional policy goals. This review raises pertinent issues that informed the selection of interviewees and the questions to be addressed in the semi-structured interviews on the goals, effectiveness and coherence of Irish regional policy, the processes by which investment priorities are determined and the implications of these for the governance of regional policy at central and regional levels. To set this in context, the chapter commences by briefly tracing the evolution of regional policy in Ireland over recent decades.

Evolution of Irish regional policy

The 1950s and 1960s were a period of active regional policy in Ireland, with, for example, the Underdeveloped Areas Act in 1952 and the establishment of the Shannon Free Zone, followed by the provision of advanced factories in dispersed locations in the mid-1970s (NESC, 1997). At this time there was a proliferation of branch plant enterprises established by foreign investors, largely engaged in low- to medium-technology assembly operations (Commins, 2006).

Ireland was unaffected by the wave of decentralisation evident in many European states from the mid 1970s to the late 1980s, as the main emphasis of public policy was on dealing with Ireland's macroeconomic problems and high unemployment levels rather than on regional issues. The Regional Development Organisations established in 1969, with a co-ordination and planning role, were abolished in 1987 due to budgetary constraints (McAleer, 2007). Local development issues came to prominence in the early 1990s with the establishment of several local structures and initiatives such as LEADER, Area-based Partnerships and County Enterprise Boards, as well as the establishment of the Western Development Commission in 1997, which was, according to O'Hara (2002: 114), 'the culmination of a long process of grassroots action to highlight the relative underdevelopment of the [West] region'.

Much of the policy impetus and financial support for regional development in Ireland in recent decades has emanated from the European Union, and the establishment of both regional tiers of administration was strongly influenced by EU cohesion policy (O'Hara and Commins, 2003). This first emerged in 1987 when the Irish government created seven regional review committees for the purpose of consultation on programme preparation and the monitoring of EU expenditure in the regions. These, according to Laffan (1996: 337) were a 'pragmatic organisational and procedural adaptation of the policy process that does not amount to meaningful regionalism and decentralisation'. Similarly, Hayward (2006: 5) describes these as 'cosmetic' and as 'superficial regional structures' with limited public impact.

As recommended in the Barrington Report on Local Government Reorganisation and Reform[8] (Advisory Expert Committee, 1991), the Local Government Act 1991 made provision for the establishment of eight indirectly elected regional authorities, which finally came into effect in 1994, with strategic planning and co-ordination functions and a role in the preparation and monitoring of EU structural and cohesion funded programmes (Laffan, 2004). Their statutory role has been enhanced somewhat under the Planning and Development Act 2000 in relation to the adoption, implementation and monitoring of Regional Planning Guidelines, thus providing a linear planning hierarchy from national to county level (McAleer, 2007). Each regional authority also has a member and an alternate member on the European Committee of the Regions.

When it emerged in the late 1990s that Ireland as a single-region state would no longer qualify for Objective 1 funding, this stimulated an active engagement by regional interests in a lobby for its retention. In July 1999 the Irish government decided to divide the country into two regions for structural funds purposes – the Border, Midland and Western region, which retained full Objective 1 status, and the Southern and Eastern region, which was designated a transitional region. This decision, according to Hayward (2006), was driven by concerns for financial advantage on the part of the state rather than by a commitment to democratic regionalisation. The regional assemblies are primarily responsible for executing the managing authority functions in respect of the Regional Operational Programmes, but have limited executive powers to implement broader regional development objectives. They do have influence on the policymaking process through recommending policy direction, networking and lobbying activities and

8 The Barrington Report recommended *inter alia* that the holding of direct elections to Regional Authorities should be considered after a period of five years and that the then Department of Local Government should be renamed the Department of Regional Development, neither of which was adopted.

through their representation on various EU and National Development Plan (NDP) monitoring committees.

The establishment of the two regional assemblies in Ireland was not accompanied by any meaningful reallocation of responsibilities between the levels of government. Drawing on fiscal federalism literature,[9] Morgenroth (2000) argues that the scope for devolution of additional responsibilities to the regional assemblies is limited; he goes on to state that these assemblies may be more suitable to take on some of the roles of central government, but that if they are to be fully accountable their membership should be directly elected.

In its submission in response to the Green Paper on Local Government Reform, the BMW Regional Assembly (2008) sets out four potential additional roles that the regional assemblies could play:

1. further develop specialisation in EU structural funds programme administration
2. widen participation in EU-wide networks of regions to identify best practices
3. continue management of Inter-regional (Interreg) programmes
4. develop a formal consultation mechanism on relevant EU policy issues.

National Development Plans and the National Spatial Strategy

Irish government policy in relation to regional development has largely been expressed through successive National Development Plans and the National Spatial Strategy in recent years. These key documents are reviewed in this section.

National Development Plan 2000–2006

An ex-ante investment needs analysis carried out by the Economic and Social Research Institute (ESRI), which preceded the finalisation of the NDP, recommended an emphasis on convergence in regional productivity rather than regional income levels along with an emphasis on creating an environment in the less developed regions more conducive to high-value-added firms (Fitzgerald et al., 1999). The ESRI also proposed the development of designated growth nodes and the allocation of additional resources, through specific programmes, targeted at the less developed regions. The latter recommendation was not taken on board in the NDP.

9 Fiscal federalism focuses on achieving economic efficiency through the appropriate allocation of roles among the levels of government.

To illustrate its commitment to addressing the regional problem, the Irish government included balanced regional development as one of four core objectives of the NDP 2000–2006, established two regional assemblies to act as the designated managing authorities for the two Regional Operational Programmes (OPs) within the NDP, and committed itself to produce a National Spatial Strategy within a short timeframe.

The NDP acknowledged that more balanced development would increase prosperity in the less developed regions and reduce congestion in the more developed regions. The government's objective for regional policy as stated in the NDP (Government of Ireland, 1999: 43) was to:

> achieve more balanced regional development in order to reduce the disparities between and within the two regions and to develop the potential of both to contribute to the greatest possible extent to the continuing prosperity of the country.

The NDP (p. 42) set out the role of gateways in regional development. These are characterised by their strategic location, endowments of economic and social infrastructure, critical mass and access to domestic and international markets, and are deemed essential to the enhanced economic performance of their hinterlands.

The NDP, following the ESRI analysis, supported the development of existing gateways and the designation of a limited number of strategically placed emerging second-tier gateways, requiring sustained planned investment. It committed the Irish government to the development of a detailed spatial blueprint within two years, to serve as the basis for long-term co-ordination of major public investment decisions. Investment under the various operational programmes was to be consistent with the NDP's regional development policy.

The NDP 2000–2006 committed the government to an investment of IR£40.588bn, of which IR£27.274bn (IR£10,259 per capita) was provisioned for the S&E region and £13.313bn (IR£13,793 per capita) for the BMW region, at 1999 constant prices. The regional assemblies were given representation on each Inter-regional OP Monitoring Committee.

During the early years of the NDP, the two major strategic frameworks (i.e. where investment takes place and what types of investment are made) did not operate in tandem. The NDP was launched in 1999, with a seven-year timeframe, whereas the National Spatial Strategy (NSS) was launched in November 2002 with a 20-year time horizon. The NDP was weak in its spatial application, specifying indicative expenditure forecasts at NUTS II (Regional Assembly) level that were not always adhered to.

In their midterm review of the NDP/Community Support Framework

(CSF), Fitzgerald et al. (2003) noted some convergence towards the EU average of regional GVA in the BMW region, the narrowing of differences in unemployment rates and similarities in population growth rates in the early years of NDP. They also note the heterogeneity of regional performance within NUTS II regions and the persistent disparities in regional output and productivity. In view of the persistent gap in regional GVA and the apparent bias in reported expenditure in favour of the more developed S&E region, the ESRI perversely concluded that the NDP had had a positive impact on balanced regional development, claiming that the output disparities might have been greater in the absence of the investment under the NDP (Fitzgerald et al., 2003).

The achievement of the NDP objective of reducing disparities within and between regions is not explicitly addressed in the midterm evaluation, nor is there any reference to the failure to provide additional investment in the less developed regions, as recommended in the ex-ante report. The midterm evaluation highlighted the absence of regional differentiation, i.e. the measures in the Regional OPs were not tailored to meet specific regional needs; there were no measures in place to build critical mass in the designated gateways and hubs; and selection criteria were not taking account of the NSS.

National Spatial Strategy 2002–2020

The NSS was launched in 2002 as a 20-year blueprint, designed to enable all parts of the country to reach their potential and contribute to national prosperity. The drawing-up of the NSS was prompted by several reports, including the NESC Report on Population Distribution and Economic Development (1997), the ESRI's investment needs study (Fitzgerald et al., 1999) and the European Spatial Development Perspective (CEC, 1999). The NESC report (1997) had suggested that the role of public policy should be to develop the economic potential of all regions in the context of maximising national performance, in relation to both economic and social wellbeing. NESC (1997: 228) had recommended the development of a functional hierarchy of growth centres that would 'stimulate economic activity in their hinterlands and counteract the diseconomies that arise from extremely polarized settlement patterns'.

In introducing the NSS, the then Taoiseach, Bertie Ahern TD, stated that the strategy recognises that in order to achieve more balanced regional development, a greater share of economic activity must take place outside the Greater Dublin Area (DEHLG, 2002). The NSS sets out a framework within which gateways, hubs, other urban centres and rural areas can act together to realise more balanced regional development. The strategy states that:

> Balanced regional development requires that the full potential of each region to contribute to the overall performance of the state be developed – on a sustainable economic, social and environmental basis. (DEHLG, 2002: 10)

The NSS acknowledges that recent economic development in Ireland has been accompanied by concentrations of employment creation and sectoral specialisations in some areas, while economic weaknesses persist in others. It provides a spatial framework so that investment in access infrastructure (road, rail, air), knowledge capital (higher education and research/innovation) and public services, along with incentives in favour of inward investment, can stimulate the selected gateways to fulfil their economic potential. The NSS is also intended to set out general principles of good spatial planning practice and a framework for settlement patterns, and it sets the context for regional planning guidelines and city and county development plans. The selected gateways are to act as regional centres for the provision of advanced health, higher education and other public services.

Two key concepts underpinning the NSS are potential and critical mass. Potential is defined as:

> the capacity that an area possesses, or could in future possess, for development, arising from its endowment of natural resources, population, labour, its economic and social capital, infrastructure and its location relative to markets. (DEHLG, 2002: 12)

The second concept, critical mass:

> relates to size and concentration of population that enables a range of services and facilities to be supported. This in turn can attract and support higher levels of economic activity and improved quality of life. (DEHLG, 2002: 12)

The NSS also recognises that improved spatial planning can improve the quality of life of citizens. It calls for better land use planning and, consistent with the ESDP, it proposes more compact high-density cities in order to minimise urban sprawl. The strategy proposes that the designated gateways offer the opportunity to develop national and regional scale activities and thus lead development in their respective regions. These, along with the hubs, are intended to support the achievement of the critical mass necessary to sustain strong levels of growth in the regions.

The strategy states that regions must be competitive in order to win investment and sustain economic activity, and that achieving a critical mass of human capital underpinned by high-quality infrastructure and a favourable business environment is necessary to achieve this. Fitzgerald and Morgenroth (2006) argue that this is consistent with economic growth theory, which suggests that there is a positive correlation between productivity and population density, and that the differences in the rates of urbanisation across Ireland are quite substantial, reinforcing the need to support the development of critical mass in the selected gateways.

The NSS reaffirms the important role played by Dublin and argues that limiting Dublin's share of the growing population would be neither feasible nor desirable, while at the same time expressing concern that the Dublin area's share may become excessive. It proposes that the regions outside Dublin should be strengthened, in order to shift some of the anticipated population and employment growth to them. It recognises that there are increasing contrasts between areas encountering congestion due to a concentration of economic activity and areas experiencing under-utilisation. It also recognises the vital contribution that rural areas have to make, including the utilisation and development of their economic resources.

Fitzgerald et al. (2003: 26) have described the NSS as addressing 'a major policy vacuum in defining the long-run spatial development strategy that the NDP, along with other policies, should adhere to' and describe the NSS as the most important regional policy document since the Buchanan Report in 1968. Fitzgerald and Morgenroth (2006) propose two key policy approaches required to support the success of the NSS, namely strong land-use planning guidelines to ensure that settlement patterns are sustainable (and to facilitate public transport) and the targeting of public investment consistent with the NSS. NESC (2005) has also recognised the challenges of ensuring that the NSS is reflected in public investment decisions and highlighted the need for a deeper understanding of the economic potential of the gateways and their hinterlands by public policymakers. Following the publication of the NSS, the eight regional authorities prepared Regional Planning Guidelines which were adopted in 2004 and each regional authority hosts a Regional Planning Guidelines Implementation Committee.

The NSS marked a change in the meaning of 'balanced regional development' from reducing disparities towards developing potential. Fitzgerald et al. (2003) suggest that the attainment of regional potential as an objective of the NSS is problematic from several perspectives. First, potential does not lend itself to measurement and evaluation. Second, potential is exogenous and can change arising from public investment. Third, some regions have lower potential than others and may permanently lag behind. On this issue, Fitzgerald et al. (2003: 203) state that 'the question for policy makers then is, whether this gap should be closed and what policies will help in this'.

Morgenroth (2003a) is also critical of the absence of an understanding of the underlying mechanisms that have driven recent spatial patterns in Ireland that can be obtained through the construction of regional economic models, and states that many of the specially commissioned reports that informed the strategy were just descriptive of these forces. The NSS, according to Morgenroth, is aspirational, based on the concept of critical mass and the need for urban centres to exceed a threshold, above which they will grow faster, but this threshold has not been quantified. Morgenroth also criticises the inclusion of a multi-centre gateway in the Midlands, which is not well defined; the absence of a binding policy on one-off rural housing (subsequently published); the absence of implementation measures; the reliance on public investment to drive the NSS; and the inadequate powers of regional authorities to implement the Regional Planning Guidelines.

A further critique of the NSS is offered by Van der Kamp (2006), who considers that the population projections on which the NSS was based may have been too low and that a revised NSS is required. He also questions the capacity of Dublin to continue to accommodate existing rates of population growth.

The reliance placed on the NSS to deliver spatial balance in Ireland raises two important questions. First, and most critically, is the correlation between productivity and population density sufficiently strong and will the designated gateways be of sufficient economic mass to rebalance economic activity in Ireland? Essentially, is the NSS the correct framework on its own to achieve balanced regional development, and how much balance can it deliver? The second question is whether or not there is the political will and the institutional commitment to enforce strict planning guidelines and target investment in support of the NSS. Notwithstanding the evident political commitment to prepare and adopt the NSS, the evidence in its early years, including the outcomes of the 2006 population census (CSO, 2006), indicates that both the political will and the institutional commitment are somewhat lacking. The absence of coherence between the NSS and national investment planning has been addressed with the publication of the NDP 2007–13, as described in the next subsection.

National Development Plan 2007–13

The ex-ante evaluation that preceded the NDP 2007–13 was also carried out by the ESRI (Morgenroth and Fitzgerald, 2006) and contains a specific chapter on regional, urban and rural development. It recommended that public investment should not be considered independently from spatial development and that the NDP 2007–13 should target investment in accordance with the NSS. Fitzgerald and Morgenroth urged adherence with the Regional Planning Guidelines, in order to avoid a continuation of unsustainable development patterns.

The ESRI's ex-ante analysis acknowledges the continued imbalance in economic development patterns and the risk that excessive concentration may pose for the overall economy. The report stresses the importance of critical mass and the role of the growth centres in enhancing the economic potential of their hinterlands. The failure to recognise the heterogeneity of regions in measure selection is noted (as per midterm evaluation), as is the need to prioritise projects linked with the designated gateways and hubs, with a better focus on the NUTS III level, as more natural spatial–economic areas. The ESRI report (2006) notes the increased divergence in GVA per capita during the first half of the NDP 2000–06: the apparent negative correlation between overall national growth and dispersion in terms of GVA per capita, while income per head and regional unemployment rates had shown some convergence over the same period. The ESRI recommended the construction of a regional economic model to capture the regional impacts of investment, a more formal NSS monitoring system and the inclusion of regional development criteria in project selection, and proposed an integrated gateway investment programme with additional funds available. In terms of investment, the ESRI highlighted the need for investment in strategic secondary routes and other enabling infrastructure to strengthen the gateways and hubs. The challenge of retaining graduates and the reliance on low-added-value firms located in peripheral regions is also noted.

The NDP 2007–13 provides for an investment of €183.7bn in five priority areas:

1. economic infrastructure
2. enterprise, science and innovation
3. human capital
4. social infrastructure
5. social inclusion.

The NDP 2007–13 has seven general goals, including one of integrating regional development within the NSS framework in order to assist all regions to deliver to their maximum potential and to enhance the quality of life of all people, wherever they live. The NDP (2007: 57) includes the objective of 'achieving a better balance between the regions in terms of economic and social development' and also refers to enhanced co-ordination and coherence between investment policy and regional planning, building on regional strengths and addressing regional weaknesses. It emphasises the role of strong urban centres in stimulating regional economic growth and proposes the introduction of a €300m Gateways Innovation Fund to advance economic infrastructure and regeneration initiatives in the gateway cities and towns. Planned investments to be supported under the mainstream NDP provision for each gateway are set out.

The NDP 2007–13 addresses many of the weaknesses of its predecessor in terms of coherence with the NSS. It adopts the NSS conception of balanced regional development, emphasising the enhancement of potential. The commitment to reducing disparities is not maintained in the new NDP. While not referring to regional competitiveness explicitly, the NDP (2007: 61) does refer to supporting the 'creation of conditions necessary to extend the process of employment and productivity growth in higher value added functions to all the regions', reflecting the two primary components of revealed competitiveness. The investment strategies contained in the NDP incorporate several sectoral strategies that had already been developed, such as Transport 21; the Strategy for Science, Technology and Innovation; and the National Action Plan for Social Inclusion. The plan also incorporates commitments contained in the most recent social partnership agreement, *Towards 2016* (Government of Ireland, 2006).

The new NDP no longer provides the primary strategic basis for the determination of investment priorities for EU co-financing. These are addressed separately in the National Strategic Reference Framework (NSRF; Government of Ireland, 2007b) and detailed in three Operational Programmes (OPs), described below. Arising from this separation, the Irish government is no longer obliged to specify indicative NUTS II level allocations in the NDP and chose not to do so. The absence of a clear measurable objective for regional policy and of specified regional investment targets severely constrains the means of evaluating the outcomes of the NDP and its contribution to achieving its stated goals, relating to regional policy.

National Strategic Reference Framework (NSRF) 2007–13

Under the 2007–13 round of structural funds, both NUTS II regions in Ireland are in the Regional Competitiveness and Employment Objective (formerly Objective 2), with the BMW region qualifying as a phasing-in region. Ireland is to receive €901m, a 76% decrease on the ~€3.8bn allocation of structural and cohesion funds over the 2000–2006 period. The NSRF is required to provide a strategic framework for the allocation of the structural funding in the OPs, consistent with the Community Strategic Guidelines on Cohesion (CEC, 2006a).

The NSRF focuses on two thematic priorities for ERDF funding, to be allocated via two Regional OPs:

- innovation, knowledge and entrepreneurship
- strengthening the competitiveness and connectivity of the gateways and hubs through improved access to quality infrastructure and environmental and sustainable development.

In addition, an ESF co-financed OP is to be implemented with ring-fenced NUTS II regional allocations.

The NSRF (Government of Ireland, 2007b) identifies the added value that Ireland has gained from EU regional policy. This includes: the benefits of the programming approach; the adoption of strategic priority investments in line with EU and national policy; the enhancement of monitoring, evaluation and project assessment procedures; and the introduction of innovative approaches, e.g. partnership-based and pilot/demonstration initiatives. However, given the smaller scale of EU co-financing compared with the previous programme, and the fact that the priorities chosen were already included in the NDP and co-financed measures are pre-financed by the Irish exchequer, EU regional policy is no longer a significant determinant of regional investment priorities in Ireland.

Selected sectoral strategies

The purpose of this section is to review the visibility of regional policy in selected sectoral strategies, and to determine the extent of horizontal coherence, in particular with the objectives of the NSS. The sectoral areas focused on are transport infrastructure, enterprise development (including FDI strategies), and the Strategy for Science, Technology and Innovation.

Transport infrastructure

The strategic framework for investment in transport infrastructure is provided in the 'Transport 21' investment plan 2006–2015, launched in November 2005. The aims of Transport 21 are to increase accessibility, sustainability, capacity, usage and quality (Department of Transport, 2008). It proposes to create an enhanced roads network that will promote regional and national competitiveness; the upgrading of the public transport system, particularly in Dublin; and the further development of airports and ports. The total planned investment is €34bn over a 10-year period, accounting for a significant part of the NDP 2007–13. Over the lifetime of the framework, there will be an increased emphasis on public transport investment, with the roads to public transport ratio now at 3:2 compared with 3:1 under the NDP 2000–06.

From a regional perspective, there are commitments to:

- upgrade key national primary and secondary routes
- the phased reopening of parts of the Western Rail Corridor from Ennis to Claremorris by 2014
- develop the Atlantic Road Corridor, consistent with the development of an Atlantic Gateway
- increase funding to the regional airports in order to enhance international access to the regions
- double funding for rural transport initiatives.

It is clear that the framework has been informed by the NSS.

The Transport 21 strategy prioritises the completion of the five major inter-urban routes[10] and an upgrade of the M50 Dublin ring road up to 2010, but does not set out a clear work programme or timescale for the upgrading of the outstanding sections of other national routes, including strategic cross-radial routes thereafter; nor is there a timescale to complete the Atlantic Road Corridor (Letterkenny/Derry to Waterford). This prioritisation strengthens accessibility to Dublin from the regional cities, while inter-gateway connectivity is of secondary importance, thus further consolidating the radial transport network emanating from Dublin. The public transport provisions are weighted heavily in favour of investment in the Dublin area, although continued investment in regional rail and bus services is contained in the programme, and a new Cork city commuter rail service to Midleton is to be provided. Apart from this, there is a limited commitment to public transport within the other designated gateways.

Enterprise policy

The enterprise policy framework in Ireland is briefly reviewed here, with an emphasis on the regional aspects of the report of the Enterprise Strategy Group (2004) and the current strategies of Enterprise Ireland (2007) and of IDA Ireland.

Enterprise policy in Ireland is largely shaped by the report of the Enterprise Strategy Group, *Ahead of the Curve* (2004). This recommended a rationalisation of regulatory bodies, increased commitments to funding for research, and an extension of research tax incentives. The report endorsed a strong emphasis on knowledge and skills levels, attraction of new inward investment, introduction of initiatives to build up marketing capabilities within firms, enhancement of research and technological development capacity and support for the development of regionally based high-technology clusters. In response to the Enterprise Strategy Group's

10 The five major inter-urban routes are the M1 (Dublin to Belfast), N6 (Dublin to Galway), N7 (Dublin to Limerick), N8 (Dublin to Cork) and N9 (Dublin to Waterford).

proposals, the Department of Enterprise, Trade and Employment published an Action Plan (2004), addressing each of the report's recommendations.

The indigenous enterprise sub-programme of the NDP 2007–13 contains a range of measures that broadly reflect the Enterprise Strategy Group's report and the Action Plan. Those documents display a lack of regional differentiation in the planned actions, with no clear regional targets; this reflects a tendency towards a 'one size fits all' approach that does not address the distinctive needs of different regions.

Enterprise Ireland (EI) launched its strategy, *Transforming Irish Industry 2008–2010*, in October 2007. The EI strategy places considerable emphasis on the internationalisation of indigenous industry, through growth in export sales, stimulation of the emergence and growth of companies of scale, and an enhancement of the innovation culture of Irish-owned enterprises. The strategy has a specific objective to realise sustained and balanced regional growth and contains the target of supporting 200 new high-potential start-ups, 100 of which are to be based outside Dublin. The strategy dedicates a chapter to the stimulation of entrepreneurship and regional development and includes measures in support of local enterprise: creation of innovation-based start-ups, proactive development of client companies in all regions through the network of EI regional offices, and collaboration with the City and County Enterprise Boards and Regional Innovation Centres. The setting of a quasi-regional target for the number of high-potential start-ups reflects the spatial disparity in the rate of establishment of innovation-based start-ups with high growth potential, although this is the only measure in which EI set a regional target.

IDA Ireland, unlike Enterprise Ireland, does not publish multi-annual strategy statements. Its end of year statement for 2007 highlights the high calibre of new investments being attracted to Ireland in target sectors such as pharmaceuticals, medical technologies, financial services and ICT, with above-average wage levels. The statement refers to the 136,000 direct jobs in IDA Ireland-supported companies in the Irish economy at the end of 2007. The challenge of attracting new greenfield investments is reflected in the fact that of 114 approved investments in 2007, only 26% were by clients new to IDA Ireland. The statement refers to a 'determined national policy to establish a substantial foundation of world class science and technology', and 40% of investments were R&D-based (IDA Ireland, 2008). The statement also refers to an IDA strategy of enhanced regional development and states that 64% of investments were outside Dublin. It is not clear whether there is a target for the number of projects outside Dublin. IDA Ireland had set itself a target of 50% of jobs in greenfield investments between 2000 and 2006 to be in the BMW region, but this target was not achieved.

The statement also endorses the NSS and states that if Ireland is to achieve a large proportion of investments outside the major cities, 'all economic and social stakeholders will need to adhere to the framework on which the NSS is constructed'. It calls for a change from a local to a regional mindset (IDA Ireland, 2008). Neither the EI strategy nor the IDA statement refers to the opportunity to bring about a higher rate of business start-up and expansion in less developed regions through exploitation of the higher regional aid rates permissible under regional aid rules. It would appear that preferential grant rates are no longer considered a potent instrument of regional policy.

Science, technology and innovation strategy

The first national Strategy for Science, Technology and Innovation 2006–2013 (SSTI) was launched by the Irish government in 2006 (Department of Enterprise, Trade and Employment, 2006). The strategy sets out to grow Irish research capability and performance, linked with the goal of developing Ireland as a knowledge-based economy and with the EU's drive to become the most competitive and dynamic, knowledge-driven economic area in the world. The strategy recognises that high levels of investment in research and innovation are essential, both for economic competitiveness and to yield innovations across a wide number of sectors. The vision as defined in the strategy is that:

> Ireland by 2013 will be internationally renowned for the excellence of its research, and will be to the forefront in generating and using new knowledge for economic and social progress, within an innovation-driven culture. (Department of Enterprise, Trade and Employment, 2006: 21)

The strategy sets out how participation in the sciences and the numbers with advanced qualifications will increase. It also aims to increase the output from research institutions, participation in transnational research activity, and the quantity and quality of research undertaken in enterprises, and to establish an international profile for Ireland in terms of the excellence of its research and development activities. It details the steps required to develop a world-class research system, building on the model of competitive excellence applied in the Programme for Research in Third Level Institutions (PRTLI) and Science Foundation Ireland (SFI) programmes. It describes proposed human capital investments and delivery mechanisms to translate knowledge into jobs and growth, and proposes to upgrade the existing research infrastructure significantly, develop new research facilities and double the number of PhD graduates by 2013.

From a regional development perspective, the potential of the Institutes of Technology to develop into effective technology resources focused on collaboration with business, on the basis of applied research and technology development, is recognised. The strategy proposes to build on the research strengths in the Institutes of Technology, support networking activities, address identified industry needs and develop competence centres.

The SSTI sets out a national innovation system and implementation structures but does not propose the development of complementary regional innovation systems and structured regional implementation arrangements, at which level the interactions with business will largely take place. It has been recognised that an effective regional innovation system can facilitate interaction between all relevant actors and unlock access to sources of knowledge (CEC, 2006c). The award of institutional research funding, following international practice, is to be based on competitive excellence, with limited emphasis on building the capacity of weaker institutions. The SWOT analysis in the strategy does not identify any spatial disparities in the level of research activity or innovation at present, such as those identified in the Audit of Innovation report for the BMW Regional Assembly (CIRCA, 2004). The strategy does not propose to address any specific spatial disparities, nor does it have any region-level targets. Although the strategy is one of the pillars of the NDP, with a planned total investment of €5.9bn over seven years, it makes no reference to the NSS and does not reflect or reinforce the goals of balanced regional development as set out in the NDP.

Sources of regional divergence in Ireland

Ireland is a small open economy, with strong trading links both within and outside the EU and a high level of FDI. Ireland experienced strong growth in economic output from the early 1990s to 2008. This has been attributed in the early years of the Celtic Tiger era to factors such as FDI, EU regional policy, EU integration, improved fiscal management, availability of a highly skilled labour force, stable social partnership arrangements and a favourable corporation tax regime (MacSharry and White, 2000).

In spite of its small size, widening regional disparities, as measured by GVA per capita, have been evident within Ireland in recent decades. This means that some regions account for an increasing share of national output, indicating a gradual process of economic concentration. The widely held view that regional disparities will always be smaller in small countries has been challenged by Felsenstein and Portnov (2005: 656), who state that 'there is no strong *a priori* case to expect small developed countries to be any more equitable than larger countries'. They argue that centralisation and concentration of political power are features of small countries, and the existence in many cases of one dominant metropolitan area (i.e., a mono-centric state) limits the potential for significant interregional spillover effects.

Several economists have attributed the evident regional output disparities in Ireland to productivity differentials (Boyle et al., 1999; O'Leary, 2002; Morgenroth, 2007a). Such disparities, they found, result from differences in sectoral productivity levels and, to some extent, from regional differences in the sectoral distribution of employment, i.e. the structure of the regional economies. The latter is important because shifting employment from low-productivity to higher productivity sectors, even without increasing the overall employment rate or the level of productivity within sectors, yields a gain in income and productivity overall (CEC, 2006b).

The sources of convergence and divergence in living standards at NUTS II level in Ireland from 1960 to 1999 were analysed by O'Leary (2002). Using the σ-convergence (coefficient of variation) measure over three time periods, he found that there was strong convergence in living standards in the 1960 to 1979 period due to relative productivity improvements and structural change (i.e. a shift from agriculture to manufacturing and service employment) in the poorer regions. In the 1979 to 1993 period there was a reversal of this trend, due primarily to productivity gains being somewhat higher in the wealthier regions. This divergent effect would have been stronger without the convergent effect of structural change. In the third period studied, 1993 to 1999, which coincided with the early years of the Celtic Tiger era, O'Leary found that demographic factors such as the employment rate, labour force participation rate and age dependency rate, along with productivity gains, positively influenced growth and a widening of regional disparities in living standards. Thus, a demographic dividend and productivity growth, and to a lesser extent structural change, drove the economic disparities during the Celtic Tiger years (O'Leary, 2002).

In 2007, O'Leary extended his analysis of regional GVA to the 1999–2003 period, and found that the divergence in regional GVA, which became pronounced during the Celtic Tiger era, had continued into the early years of the new millennium. Morgenroth (2007a) examined the evolution of productivity differences across Ireland's regions, and found that productivity growth in the manufacturing and construction sectors in particular drove the regional divergence apparent between 1991 and 2003.

Fitzgerald et al. (2003) refer to the sectoral composition of regional economies as being one of the most important determinants of Irish regions' relative economic success. This is supported by Morgenroth (2007), who argues that a shift away from primary production towards modern sectors supports convergence. In an earlier paper, Morgenroth (2006) found that regions with greater sectoral diversity (low specialisation) had higher productivity, contrary to some new economic geography models which predict that industries will concentrate to avail of increasing returns to scale. Morgenroth concludes that the differential rates of decline in sectoral specialisation across Ireland's regions may have contributed to regional divergence in economic output.

Morgenroth (2006) also showed that labour force participation rates have converged considerably in recent years, and predicted that structural change will be less significant in future and that productivity growth will be the most critical factor determining regional convergence. In a later paper, Morgenroth (2007) found that productivity at regional level is positively correlated with average plant size, regional share of employment in foreign-owned firms, proportion of administrative and service-type employment, output per production unit and output per worker. Fitzgerald and Morgenroth (2006: 80) found that national growth had not lifted all regions in relative terms but that there had been some convergence in recent years in total per capita personal income and a marked reduction and convergence in unemployment rates.

Notwithstanding the strong empirical evidence of widening productivity differentials as the primary source for widening regional disparities, it is also arguable that such disparities were allowed to happen due to the absence of focused coherent regional policies. Related to this is the fact that regional concerns did not feature prominently in the social partnership process and regional interests are not among the 'community of social partners' as described by Boucher and Collins (2003: 303). Similarly, Laffan (2004: 8) notes that partnership is weak at regional level 'because of the weakness of the regional tier of government'. Dublin and its hinterland have been the dominant driver of economic development in the Republic of Ireland and have attracted substantial inward investment from abroad and skilled workers from the rest of the country. Other urban centres demonstrate weaker agglomeration effects. Regional convergence is therefore unlikely in the absence of other cities of equal prominence to Dublin.

There is a growing interest internationally in the regional foundations of competitiveness and the creation of competitive regional milieux (Maillet, 1997). In Ireland, limited consideration is given to subnational competitiveness factors, and there would appear to be a limited appreciation of the underlying agglomeration processes at work in Ireland (Morgenroth, 2003b). For example, there has been no official acknowledgement in Ireland of the regional impact of the concentration of research activity and the localised spillover of commercial innovations into high-value enterprises in a small number of centres, although this phenomenon has been acknowledged elsewhere (CEC, 2006a). The decentralisation of economic policy that is quite evident elsewhere in Europe has not occurred to any great extent in Ireland.

The interventionist central state reallocating resources to underperforming regions may no longer be an appropriate development model. The worst-case scenario for Ireland's weakest regions, from a regional balance perspective, involves increased global exposure, declining competitive assets and a central state decreasingly inclined to intervene.

Other underlying factors have been identified, including the proportion of the population with third-level qualifications, the relative strength of regional innovation capacity, the concentration of university-based research, the stock of public infrastructure and the degree of urbanisation. All of these lead to mutually reinforcing path-dependent processes (Fitzgerald and Morgenroth, 2006; Morgenroth, 2007a). The pattern of transport infrastructure investment under the NDP 2000–2006 has also potentially strengthened the dominance of Dublin over the other designated gateways (growth centres) in recent years.

Regional socioeconomic trends

This section briefly reviews selected trends in relation to population, output (GVA), disposable income, employment status, sectoral employment and regional innovation. Due to the heterogeneous nature of the NUTS II regions, data at NUTS III level are used where available.

Population

The population of the Republic of Ireland grew by 8.0% over the 1996–2002 intercensal period, and by a further 8.1% over the 2002–2006 period (see Figure 4.1). The 2006 census (CSO, 2006) found positive population trends in many previously underdeveloped counties, but also indicated that urban sprawl continued to be a feature of new settlement patterns. The population of the Mid-East region grew by 18.8% over the 1996–2002 period, and by a further 15.1% in 2002–2006, while that of the Midlands region grew at above-average rates of 9.6% and 11.5% over the same periods. The population of County Dublin (the Dublin NUTS III region) grew by just 6.1% and 5.6%. Combining the Dublin and Mid-East regions (Greater Dublin Area) gives an above-average growth of 9.2% over the first period and a growth of 8.1%, equal to the national average, over the second period. It is also interesting to note that the population of the NUTS II BMW region grew by 9.0% in the 2002–2006 intercensal period, while the Southern and Eastern NUTS II region grew by 7.8%, somewhat below the national average.

Figure 4.1: Population of Irish regions 1996–2006 (Source: Central Statistics Office, 2006)

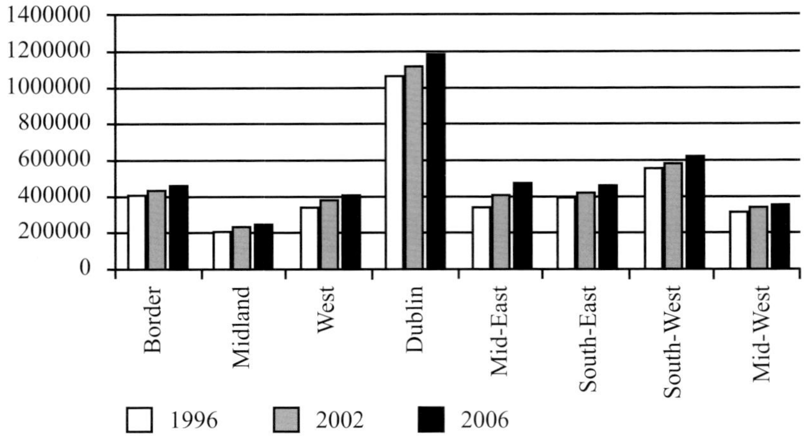

The 2006 census results also showed that population growth rates were below average in several of the designated gateways. Fitzgerald and Morgenroth (2006) express concerns about this and also about the implications of the CSO-forecasted population settlement patterns, particularly for the Midlands region, where population growth does not appear to be accompanied by economic development. This, they claim, will lead to unsustainable commuting patterns and an undermining of the NSS.

The population of the Republic of Ireland is expected to reach 5 million by 2021 (CSO, 2005). This provides an opportunity to rebalance unsustainable settlement patterns with a corresponding requirement to put the necessary economic, social and environmental infrastructure in place, within a robust spatial planning framework. The NSS, Regional Planning Guidelines and the County Development Plans are intended to provide this framework.

Regional output (GVA)

Figure 4.2 tracks the growth in GVA per capita over the 2000–2005 period. The Border, Midland and West NUTS III regions consistently underperform on this measure. The NDP (2007) acknowledges that GVA per capita grew by 51.2% in the S&E region between 1999 and 2004 and by 49.9% in the BMW region over the same period, thus indicating that the BMW region is producing a declining share of national output. Notably, the coefficient of variation in regional GVA was 0.18 in 1995 but rose to 0.27 in 2002 and dropped to 0.25 in 2005, indicating σ-divergence up to 2002 and slight σ-convergence between 2002 and 2005. The lowest performing region, the Midlands, stood at 59% of the highest region (Greater Dublin Area) in 1995. This dropped to 51% in 1999 and rose to 54% in 2005.

Figure 4.2: Trends in regional GVA per capita 2000–2005 (Source: Central Statistics Office, County Incomes and Regional GDP, 2008)

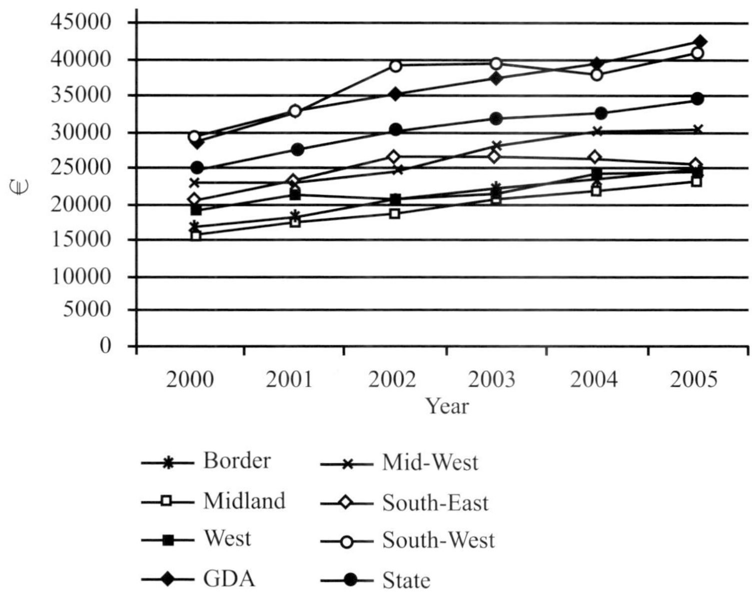

GDP per capita, the almost universally applied measure of economic wellbeing, is not regarded as entirely appropriate to Ireland as a measure of living standards and productivity, due to the extent of profit repatriations and transfer pricing by foreign-owned firms (O'Leary, 1999; Fitzgerald and Morgenroth, 2006). However, in the absence of a more accurate and consistently available measure of real regional output, along the lines of 'Gross Regional Product' which is a complex measure to obtain, it is difficult to see how the trends in regional output per capita can be tracked in a satisfactory manner and appropriate conclusions drawn.

Disposable incomes

The poorest performing regions over the 1995–2005 period in terms of disposable incomes were the Midlands and South-East. The coefficient of variation in regional disposable incomes was of a much lower magnitude than that of regional GVA, at 0.071 in 1995, rising to 0.087 in 1999 and falling to 0.071 in 2005. The general trend over the period was one of σ-convergence from 1999 to 2005. The Midlands region had a disposable income per capita of 80% of the Dublin level in 1995, which fell to 76% in 1999 and rose to 82% in 2004 (Figure 4.3).

Figure 4.3: Trends in regional disposable incomes per capita 2000–2005 (Source: Central Statistics Office, 2008)

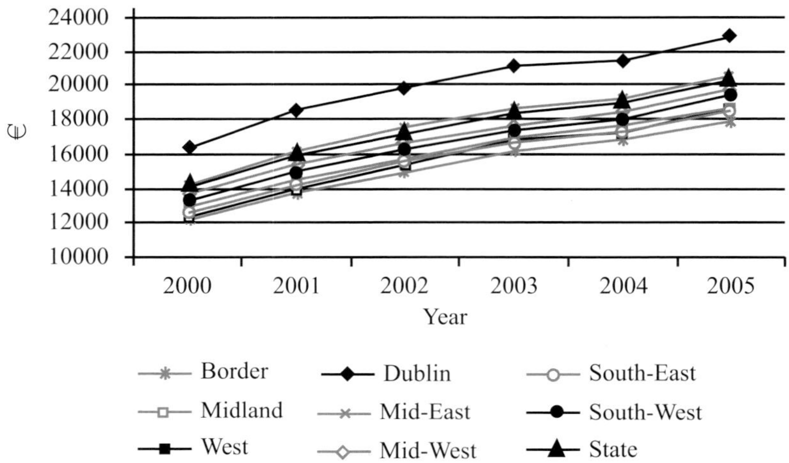

The three factors that account for the differing gaps in GVA and disposable income per capita at regional level have been identified by Fitzgerald et al. (2003) as:

1. the effect of the tax and welfare systems and farm transfer payments on equalising disposable incomes to some extent
2. the effect of inter-regional commuting on output levels where commuters work and on disposable income levels where they live
3. the distortion of output levels caused by transfer pricing and profit shifting.

The increasingly prevalent phenomenon of long-distance commuting is both inefficient from an economic perspective and unsustainable environmentally.

The impact of the Irish fiscal system on relative income differences was analysed by Morgenroth (2007b), who found that the Irish fiscal system is redistributive, with the two richest regions (Dublin and the South-West) contributing more in tax revenues than they receive in public expenditure while still receiving an above-average share per capita.

Regional employment

Table 4.1 sets out the employment status of all persons over 15 years of age for each of the NUTS II and NUTS III regions and at state level in the third quarter (Q3) of 1997 and 2007. The most notable difference over the period reviewed is the 46% increase in the number employed at national level. At NUTS II level, the increase is 55% in the BMW region and 43% in the S&E region. The highest increases occurred in the Mid-East and Midland regions, at 69.1% and 63.9% respectively. The lowest increase was in the Dublin region at 32%. These figures are taken from the CSO Quarterly National Household Survey (QNHS) and are based on place of residence. The data correlate with Figure 4.1, which indicated higher rates of population increase in the Mid-East and Midland regions.

Table 4.1: Persons over 15 years classified by ILO economic status at NUTS II, NUTS III and national levels (Source: Central Statistics Office, 2007)

	No. employed (000)		**No. unemployed (000)**		**Unemployment rate (%)**		**Participation rate (%)**	
	Q3 97	Q3 07	Q3 97	Q3 07	Q3 97	Q3 07	Q3 97	Q3 07
Border	144.3	222.4	21.9	15.8	13.2	6.6	53.5	62.2
Midland	77.3	126.7	8.3	5.0	9.7	3.8	54.3	64.3
West	135.4	206.0	14.7	10.0	9.8	4.6	55.1	64.0
BMW	357.0	555.1	44.9	30.8	11.2	5.3	54.3	63.3
Dublin	472.5	623.9	56.4	31.8	10.7	4.8	62.5	66.1
Mid-East	151.6	256.4	14.0	10.3	8.4	3.9	60.6	68.8
Mid-West	125.2	173.4	11.9	9.8	8.7	5.4	56.2	62.9
South-East	148.2	225.6	19.2	11.5	11.5	4.8	55.6	63.0
South-West	213.0	311.7	24.7	13.1	10.4	4.0	55.9	64
S&E	1,110.7	1,590.9	126.3	76.5	10.2	4.6	59.2	65.3
State	1,467.7	2,146.0	171.2	107.3	10.4	4.8	57.9	64.8

In terms of unemployment, the overall trend has been a significant decline in both the numbers and the rate of unemployment in the labour force up to 2007. It is noteworthy that the Border region had the highest unemployment rate (13.2%) in Q3 1997 and again in Q3 2007 (6.6%), while the Mid-East region had the lowest rate in Q3 1997 (8.4%) and again in Q3 2007 (3.9%).

The gap in participation rate, e.g. 68.8% in the Mid-East region in 2007 compared with 62.2% in the Border region, is one of the contributors to the gap in output per capita reviewed earlier.

This analysis is consistent with that of Walsh (2006), who reviewed the comparative labour force performance of the Irish NUTS III regions, particularly over the Celtic Tiger period.[11] He acknowledges that disparities in regional GVA widened over the period under review, but questions the current concern with the Irish regional problem, citing evidence of convergence in unemployment rates, consistent increases in labour force participation rates and the relatively stable share of national employment, in each region. Walsh argues that Ireland's regions have had relatively stable spatial distributions of population and employment, that wage differentials and income per capita did not widen during this period, and that all Irish regions participated in the economic boom of the Celtic Tiger period. Walsh did not carry out a sectoral analysis of employment across regions or explore why GVA per capita differentials widened during the period under review, or why income per capita differences did not narrow over a period of unprecedented economic prosperity. He acknowledges, however, that the impact of a recession may be felt very differently across the regions.

Sectoral composition of employment

The sectoral composition of employment at NUTS II regional level in 1997 and 2007 is set out in Table 4.2. The key changes over that period are the increases in employment in both regions across most sectors, with the exception of agriculture and other production industries, and the large increases in construction and public sector employment. The comparatively high proportion of employment in financial and business services, a high value-added sector, in the S&E region is also notable. In view of the critical importance of the sectoral composition of regional economies as a determinant of Irish regions' economic performance (see Fitzgerald et al., 2003), the sectoral profile at the time exposed the BMW region in particular in the event of an economic downturn.

The BMW Audit of Innovation (CIRCA, 2004) found a low incidence of ICT, high-potential start-up (HPSU) and internationally traded service companies in the region. Table 4.3 gives an indication of the geographic spread of ICT and biotechnology companies in Ireland, of which only 9.9% were located in the BMW region in 2003.

---

11 Walsh reviewed disposable income indices 1995–2003, regional employment shares and unemployment rates 1988–2005, and population trends 1971–2002.

Table 4.2: Sectoral composition of employment at NUTS II level, 1997 and 2007 (Source: Central Statistics Office, 2007)

Sector	**1997**		**2007**	
	BMW	S&E	BMW	S&E
Agriculture, forestry & fishing	57.2	77.4	45.8	72.1
Other production industries	82.1	216.1	79.2	213.8
Construction	32.4	89.9	83.6	199
Wholesale & retail services	45.1	162.2	80.7	228.9
Hotels & restaurants	23.2	69.9	38.9	91.2
Transport, storage & communications	14.2	68.8	24.2	98
Financial & business services	27.6	145.3	47.5	248.8
Public administration & defence	15.3	53.9	30.2	82
Education	20.9	71.7	33.1	98.2
Health	28.7	85.1	60.4	158.3
Other	17.7	69.7	29.1	92.9

Table 4.3: Large ICT and biotech companies in Ireland, 2003 (Source: CIRCA, 2004)

Region	**ICT**		**Pharmaceutical & Chemical**		**Total**	
Border	3	2.7%	6	7.4%	9	4.6%
Midlands	1	0.9%	2	2.5%	3	1.7%
West	6	5.4%	1	1.2%	7	3.6%
BMW Region	10	9.0%	9	11.1%	19	9.9%
S&E Region	101	91.0%	72	88.9%	173	90.1%
Total	111	100%	81	100%	192	100%

The above findings are consistent with those of the Expert Group on Future Skills Needs (EGFSN, 2006), which assessed the presence in each of the NUTS III regions of six key sectors that account for a high share of high-added-value exports. It found for example that the BMW region hardly participated at all in the substantial growth in employment in the ICT sector, but fared better in medical devices and engineering. The EGFSN also found a clear bias in higher skilled occupations towards Dublin.

Regional innovation

The Forfás Innovation Survey (2006b) provided a regional analysis of innovation activity by firms on a NUTS II regional basis. The survey found that innovation activity is higher overall among firms in the S&E region (52.6% of firms) compared with the BMW region (50.8% of firms). The data are broken down in the survey report by type of firm, as shown in Figure 4.4. This shows that the difference in innovation activity rates is greater in the services sector than in the industrial sector.

Figure 4.4: Regional sectoral innovation rates 2006 (Source: Forfás, 2006b)

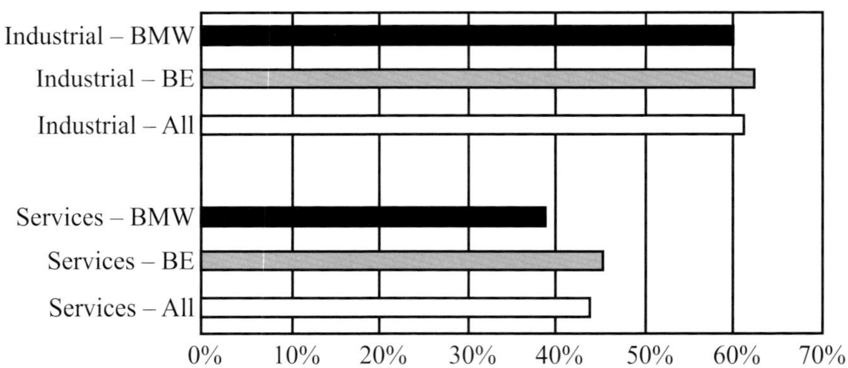

One important barrier to developing R&D and innovation in the BMW region is the fact that there is only one university (NUI Galway) and two major research institutes (the Marine Institute and Teagasc) in the region, all of which are located in the vicinity of Galway city. One way in which this barrier can be overcome is through strengthening the role of the Institutes of Technology (IoTs) by developing more applied research and fostering greater linkages with industry, as advocated in the OECD's higher education review (2006). Collins (2002) argued that while Ireland had been very successful in the information economy, particularly as a prime location for software-exporting activities, it had been less successful as an information society, with relatively low levels of PC usage and broadband access, which are among the key enablers of innovation.

Drawing on the results of a survey of 184 established high-technology businesses in Ireland, Jordan and O'Leary (2005) found that notwithstanding the large investment in research and development infrastructure in Irish universities, and the policy emphasis on establishing business networks, the levels of interaction between firms, third-level colleges and innovation support agencies was quite low. They also found that firm interactions with other group companies, customers and suppliers were predominantly over long distances. Jordan and O'Leary (2005) suggest that a greater emphasis needs to be placed on building industry-relevant applied research capacity in third-level institutions and on supports for in-company research and development.

Other factors

There are numerous other fields that indicate disparate performance across the regions of Ireland. These include the availability of enabling infrastructure such as broadband, which displays a distinct urban/rural bias whereby the more rural regions perform most poorly (Forfás, 2006a). Tourism industry earnings and visitor numbers also indicate disparate regional performance. In 2007, the Dublin region accounted for 38.3% of total overseas visitors, a 7.7 percentage point increase in share over the period 1999–2007 (Fáilte Ireland, 2008).

Chapter conclusions

The Irish government has recognised regional disparities as a problem in successive National Development Plans and in the National Spatial Strategy and has devised investment policies to address the issue. However, the establishment of regional structures has not entailed the devolution of significant additional responsibilities to the regional level. The goal of regional policy has shifted from one of reducing disparities to fulfilling the potential of each region to contribute to overall national development. Nevertheless, the persistence of regional disparities in regional output and the continued spatial concentration of high-value-added economic activities would indicate that the policy response has not been entirely effective to date. It is evident that the goals of regional policy, as set out in the NSS and reinforced in the NDP 2007–13, are more apparent in some strategies (e.g. transport infrastructure) than in others (e.g. science and technology), indicating that policy coherence has not been fully attained.

The sources of economic disparities have been attributed to productivity differentials, industry structure, demographic factors and the greater presence of high-value economic activities in some regions than in others. This has been compounded by the location decisions of multinational enterprises, which account for a disproportionate level of GDP in some regions, and other underlying factors such as the concentration of innovation and human resource capacity, agglomeration economies accruing to larger cities and the stock of public infrastructure. The concentration of high-value-added activities in a small number of urban centres is likely to persist in the absence of countervailing policies.

Different measures of regional performance reveal differing findings on the extent and nature of regional disparities in Ireland. Measures of output (GDP/GVA) per capita, the most commonly used indicator of economic performance notwithstanding the limitations of its applicability to Ireland, indicate continued disparities. On the other hand, measures of regional labour market conditions indicate some convergence up to 2007. Measures of disposable incomes reveal some disparities, which are in decline, while measures of settlement show that all regions experienced unprecedented levels of population growth up to 2006, but indicate that the largest increases have taken place in the Dublin commuter belt, inconsistent with the objectives of the NSS.

Arising from the above findings, it would appear that challenges remain in terms of achieving greater balance of economic output levels and productivity, research and innovation performance and increasing the combined population share of the designated gateways, as a counterbalance to Dublin. These issues have been incorporated into the interviews of key respondents, analysed in the next chapter.

5

Findings and Discussion

This chapter sets out the findings of the semi-structured interviews, following the sequence of the issues set out in the interview guide. Four categories of leading personnel were interviewed, representing government and national agencies, subnational public bodies, selected academic experts and social partner bodies. The selection, recording and transcription of interviewees, the focus of the semi-structured interviews and the analysis of the transcripts followed a recursive iterative format. This is consistent with the principles of qualitative data analysis in which initial findings were used to refine and focus subsequent interviews and to explore the key issues and concepts that emerged as significant common themes as the interviews progressed.

The findings set out in this chapter are discussed in the light of the insights derived from the literature review in Chapter 2 and are correlated, where applicable, with the analysis set out in Chapter 4. An anonymised code is used in footnotes throughout the chapter to attribute quotations and paraphrased statements to interviewees without breaching confidentiality. Details within a quotation that may identify an interviewee have been removed. Numbers in parentheses indicate the number of interviewees that supported a particular viewpoint.

Rationale for Irish regional policy

The first question asked at all interviews related to the rationale or basis for regional policy in Ireland. Consideration of rationale is important from two perspectives. First, it expounds the fundamental reasons why public policy intervention is justified, and second, the rationale can determine the basis for the selection of appropriate public policy intervention. A public policy domain for which there is a weak rationale, or in which the policy interventions are inconsistent with the rationale, could be judged to be an unnecessary or an incoherent public policy.

Several potential rationales for regional policy intervention, ranging from social equity to market efficiency to administrative efficiency, were reviewed in Chapter 2. It was argued that excessive regional imbalances can undermine national economic prosperity, and that policies that address market failures and bring under-utilised resources into production can raise the economic potential of regions and countries.

All interviewees stated that Ireland should have a regional policy, although the justifications cited for this differed somewhat. There were no discernible differences in the responses from each of the four categories of interviewee. The need to counter disparities in economic development and the need for a counterbalance to Dublin and the east coast were the most common responses, as typified by the following response from a government agency interviewee:[12] 'I think we need to have counterbalances to the growth that has taken place in Dublin and as balanced as we can to drive that across Ireland'. A further rationale suggested was the avoidance of overdevelopment in some areas and underdevelopment of others, so that overall national economic potential and wellbeing could be optimised. This was expressed by an academic interviewee,[13] as follows:

> The country is not evenly developed spatially and this has implications for efficiency. At the moment we are over-using the East and we're under-using the West, if I can put it in that blunt way.

Other responses included the need to address market failures that can be regionally specific, and the need for spatially sensitive regulation. Consistent with Martin (2000), for example, an academic interviewee[14] stated that 'market failure is based around the notion that there are resources that are not properly utilised'. Administrative efficiency as a rationale for the subnational organisation of public services was mentioned by only one interviewee.[15]

A minority of interviewees (seven) proposed equity arguments as a justification for regional policy. The spatial incidence of social exclusion was identified by a small number (two) as a basis for area-based or regional policy interventions, and the need for equality of access to services, especially health services, also received some mentions; for example, a regional interviewee[16] stated that:

> All people in a region should have equality whether it be equality of opportunity, equality of services or equality of economic and social development and also the equality of potential for employment.

Some respondents questioned the relevance of regional policy to meeting

---

12 Interviewee 12.
13 Interviewee 2.
14 Interviewee 21.
15 Interviewee 17.
16 Interviewee 17.

redistributive policy objectives; a regional interviewee[17] stated that regional policy was not as effective an equity instrument as other social policies. The role of 'place' and the need for public policies and investment programmes to have a spatial expression were mentioned by two interviewees.[18]

Two regional interviewees[19] stated that the emphasis in highlighting the need for regional policy should be on its role in increasing overall national wellbeing, rather than simply easing development pressures on Dublin, because, it was stated, if the current development pressures on Dublin ease, the impetus for regional policy to support economic development elsewhere in the state may recede:[20]

> In the medium term, if the pressure on Dublin eases, and what we're seeing proposed in terms of transport investment in the new NDP may do that, the impetus for regional policy may decline even further.

The argument, it was stated, should be focused on how underperforming regions constrain national potential, as highlighted by O'Leary (2003), and that historic under-investment provided a rationale for discriminatory investment in favour of underdeveloped regions.[21]

A social partner interviewee[22] expressed concern that an over-emphasis on balance risked weakening the dynamic of the Dublin region. This echoes the issues raised by NESC (1997), and by Morgenroth (2000) in relation to the potential of regional policy to divert economic activity away from the region that offers the best prospects for success, whereby the economy would lose out on the benefits of agglomeration.

Two further rationales identified that are likely to become more evident in the future were the need for regional policy to counter the disparate effects of globalisation[23] on locations, and the likely differential effects of climate change on regions in Ireland.[24] An academic interviewee[25] stated that the rationale of maximising EU receipts no longer applied to Ireland and evinced that the current emphasis of regional policy is based on redistribution rather than growth, due to the fact that it is highly politicised. This would appear to be inconsistent with the predominant rationale that can be derived from the interviews.

---

17 Interviewee 3.
18 Interviewees 3 and 24.
19 Interviewees 9 and 17.
20 Interviewee 9.
21 Interviewee 4.
22 Interviewee 6.
23 Interviewee 19.
24 Interviewee 6.
25 Interviewee 20.

The responses to this question would suggest that there is a strong rationale for regional policy in Ireland, based on the need to counter disparities and avoid the economic costs of overdevelopment and underdevelopment. The locus of the regional policy debate in Ireland is shifting from one of 'regional equity' to 'regional efficiency', consistent with a diminution of EU-influenced cohesion as the overarching goal of Irish regional policy. The need for public services to cohere spatially was also raised frequently, suggesting a particular co-ordinating role for region-level public bodies.

Current goals and principal features of Irish regional policy

The second theme on the interview guide included the related issues of the goals and principal features of Irish regional policy. For the purpose of clarity, these are dealt with separately here.

Current goals

Interviewees were asked what they considered the current goals of regional policy to be. Goals are important for a number of reasons: they define the overall policy objectives and direction, and they have a motivational effect by setting out the desired policy outcomes. Clear goals are also the foundations for strategy formulation and policy evaluation, and the process of goal definition requires that conflicting policy objectives be resolved (Parr, 2001). A clearly defined and consistently understood goal is therefore an important element of policy coherence.

The most frequent response to this question, across all groups, was to cite the goal set out in the NSS, i.e. to enable all regions to fulfil their potential and, in so doing, to optimise national performance. A government interviewee[26] expressed it as follows:

> regional policy in Ireland is about enabling all regions in Ireland to fulfil their maximum potential, not only in terms of the benefits that will accrue to regions themselves, but also to ensure that the national performance is optimised.

There was a high degree of consistency in the responses of the central government and agency interviewees to this question. The alignment of the new NDP with the NSS (as discussed in the previous chapter) had moved the focus away from reducing disparities, which was described by a regional

26 Interviewee 1.

interviewee[27] as 'the level playing field approach' and towards enhancing the economic performance of regions and, in particular, the competitiveness of the gateways.[28] This had reinforced competitiveness as the predominant goal, according to some interviewees.

The next most frequent response, notably coming from several academic interviewees,[29] was that the current goals for regional policy are aspirational or rhetorical statements, or are unclear, with unidentifiable targets. Some interviewees questioned the feasibility of having precise goals for public policies and stated that public policy goals are not always amenable to measurement, notwithstanding the desirability of having clearly defined policy outcomes; for example, a social partner interviewee[30] stated that 'in a lot of public policy, goals and means are a bit more interactive and recursive than we might imagine'. A further response was that policy inputs were clearly measurable, but the outcomes were not.[31]

The attainment of balanced regional development as the current goal was mentioned by some interviewees, expressed in terms such as[32] 'no region left behind'. An academic interviewee[33] commented that although the official goal had shifted to raising the potential of all areas, in the public mind the goal is still about ensuring that 'everywhere gets a fair share of the cake', a point echoed by a regional interviewee[34] as 'expenditure balancing'. Balance was described by another regional interviewee[35] as a political concept but not useful as a policy tool. It was argued that identifying potential for growth and maximising each region's contribution was a challenging but more useful goal. The political system in Ireland was described as responsive by a central government interviewee,[36] who stated that wide disparities in any field were usually addressed.

The limitations of using the concept of potential, due to its endogenous, changeable and unmeasurable nature, were highlighted by an academic respondent.[37] Several interviewees[38] acknowledged that potentials do differ and that having equal levels of productivity is not practicable. This corresponds to the critique of the spatial strategy, particularly that of

27 Interviewee 13.
28 Interviewee 9.
29 Interviewees 19, 20 and 23.
30 Interviewee 6.
31 Interviewee 20.
32 Interviewee 7.
33 Interviewee 22.
34 Interviewee 17.
35 Interviewee 3.
36 Interviewee 1.
37 Interviewee 23.
38 Interviewees 1, 3, 18 and 23.

Morgenroth (2003a), as outlined in Chapter 4. An academic interviewee[39] stated that the concepts of regional balance and regional potential are incompatible, and that unbalanced growth based on potential may generate higher levels of output overall, which would then facilitate greater levels of redistribution.

Attaining sustainable settlement patterns[40] and the social objectives of regional policy[41] were each mentioned just once. Finally, a social partner interviewee[42] stated that politicians and public policymakers are not motivated by clear goals; rather, they respond to pressure. Concepts such as cohesion, convergence and polycentric spatial structuring were not cited frequently in the interviews, which is perhaps not surprising as these terms have not featured prominently in public discourse.

Overall, it can be deduced from the interviewees that the National Spatial Strategy has largely set the agenda in terms of defining the overarching goal for regional policy in Ireland. The alignment of the new NDP with the NSS has reinforced this. Enhancing the potential of each region to maximise its contribution to overall national competitiveness, by focusing on designated growth centres, rather than achieving balanced regional development, was the response of a majority of interviewees. This was defined by an academic interviewee[43] as a 'shift from balance of resources to balance of opportunities' and from a needs-based approach to accentuating potential. Balanced regional development was perceived by some as a populist goal, useful politically but not practically.[44] The broad (although not universal) acceptance of one clearly articulated goal is positive from a policy coherence perspective. Notwithstanding the emerging consensus on the definition of the goal, the lack of measurable objectives or targets does not lend itself to precise evaluation of the effectiveness of Irish regional policy.

Principal features of Irish regional policy

Under the second theme on the interview guide, interviewees were also asked to identify the principal features of regional policy in Ireland. The purpose of including this question was to capture the scope of the policy domain as understood by the four categories of interviewee. It was also intended to identify its interaction, and complementarities, with other related policy domains.

39 Interviewee 23.
40 Interviewee 10.
41 Interviewee 13.
42 Interviewee 8.
43 Interviewee 21.
44 Interviewee 3.

Regional policy in Ireland was described as consisting of the NSS as the planning framework and public investment through the NDP and sectoral strategies as the vehicle.[45] From a central government perspective,[46] the NSS was described as the 'essence of regional policy' and other public policies were viewed as complementary to that. Public investment from a regional policy perspective was viewed as building the capacity of regions. Some respondents[47] stated that there was an over-emphasis on the gateway and hubs at the expense of other areas.

The limitations of regional policy as a framework policy informing and interacting with other public policy domains, rather than a policy programme with its own budget, were identified by two interviewees.[48] Some interviewees stated that sectoral policy objectives always took precedence, but that sectoral policy domains outside regional policy *per se* (e.g. health policy and education policy) make a substantial difference to regional wellbeing, although they are often poorly co-ordinated at regional level; for example, a social partner interviewee[49] stated that 'a goal of regional policy might be met significantly by ensuring that educational opportunities are equal and that health opportunities are equal'. Regional policy was described by some interviewees as not being embedded in the political or administrative system, and as subservient to national sectoral policy.[50] Overall support for regional policy was described as weak, with no electoral imperative and no vocal regional advocates, as expressed by one social partner interviewee:[51] 'frankly, the push for regional development is weak enough, it is certainly not connected to any power brokers on the ground'. It was also stated that the political culture favoured localism,[52] which was not conducive to political buy-in for regional policy.

The use of passive policies (e.g. avoidance of negative regional impacts) as well as proactive instruments (e.g. public investment) was proposed by an academic interviewee.[53] The need for proofing of the strategies of enterprise agencies against regional policy goals was identified by a central government interviewee,[54] while a regional interviewee[55] decried the 'one size fits all' undifferentiated approach adopted by several national agencies.

---

45 Interviewee 21.
46 Interviewee 1.
47 Interviewees 9 and 21.
48 Interviewees 2 and 3.
49 Interviewee 6.
50 Interviewees 3, 6 and 9.
51 Interviewee 5.
52 Interviewee 24.
53 Interviewee 22.
54 Interviewee 2.
55 Interviewee 4.

The principle of funding differentiation in the previous NDP, and the availability of higher regional aid rates under EU competition rules, were cited as features of regional policy by some interviewees,[56] but these had not been particularly effective as concomitant policy differentiation had not been put in place.[57] One regional interviewee[58] stated that there had been an over-emphasis on grants, which had created a dependency culture in less developed regions:

> in areas where there has been a high level of government intervention through grants etc., it has created a high level of dependency culture and in some respects that has stifled enterprise.

The trend towards urban-centred inward investment and the need to respond to the demands of urban-seeking employees was noted by two interviewees.[59] The government's decentralisation programme was viewed by a central government interviewee[60] as an element of regional policy, to the extent that it involved the deconcentration of the location of central government offices, although another interviewee[61] described the decentralisation process as a 'dissipated opportunity' as it had not been well aligned with the NSS. The redistributive effects of the tax and welfare system were also cited as important elements of regional policy.[62] A central government interviewee[63] noted that environmental sustainability did not receive sufficient attention. Environmental sustainability was subsequently raised by some interviewees[64] as a potential future driver of regional policy. It is noteworthy that there were limited or no references to some of the regional policy instruments reviewed in the literature review, in particular the diffusion of science and technology and human capital policies.

In summary, the NSS features prominently as the principal framework of regional policy in Ireland, with public investment intended to be complementary to this. Regional policy was viewed as secondary to sectoral policies, but it was acknowledged that sectoral policies can in their own right make a substantial contribution to regional wellbeing. Some evidence of this in enterprise policy was identified, but other policy domains were considered to be insufficiently nuanced to reflect differential regional needs.

56 Interviewees 15, 23 and 24.
57 Interviewee 9.
58 Interviewee 13.
59 Interviewees 14 and 15.
60 Interviewee 1.
61 Interviewee 15.
62 Interviewee 23.
63 Interviewee 18.
64 Interviewees 10, 22 and 24.

The absence of strong advocates for regional policy was given as one reason for the subsidiary status of regional issues in public policy. Funding differentiation was viewed as a weak instrument without policy differentiation. Decentralisation and the redistributive effects of the taxation and welfare systems were also identified as features of regional policy. The interactions of regional policy with sectoral policy domains, to ensure more effective horizontal co-ordination, requires a structured form of interaction and 'proofing' to avoid negative regional outcomes. The boundaries of the regional policy domain are not discrete and other policy domains, although centrally planned, can have substantial spatial impacts.

Effectiveness of Irish regional policy

The concept of effectiveness in the context of this study was described in Chapter 2 as the perceived adequacy of the policy to meet its intended goals as well as its success in actually doing so. Assessment of effectiveness is a measure of the functionality of policy actions in a particular domain, as well as an assessment as to whether the desired outcomes are being attained. Addressing the issue of effectiveness presupposes that policymakers 'have the measure' of what is required to achieve the intended outcomes and that the desired outcomes are clear. Interviewees were asked to state how effective they considered current regional policy to be.

The responses to this question were almost equally divided on the substantive issue of effectiveness. Although the interviewees from regional bodies largely viewed the policy as ineffective, at least one interviewee from each of the four groups was to be found on either side of the argument. On the positive side, several interviewees highlighted the economic growth that had taken place in all regions in recent years, the much improved labour market situation and population growth, and many stated that disparities had been limited, in spite of the dominance of the Greater Dublin Area. For example, a central government interviewee[65] stated that:

> I think that the fact that we're measuring over the last 15–20 years where our performance has rocketed and led Europe in various OECD tables in terms of performance has helped to improve the quality of life of all of the regions, and when you have had population growth in every single county for the first time since the 1840s, this is a sign that the country as a whole is performing.

It was also argued[66] that in the absence of regional policy, the disparities

65 Interviewee 18.
66 Interviewee 23.

would have been much greater. This is consistent with the conclusions of the midterm evaluation of the NDP/CSF (Fitzgerald et al., 2003), as discussed in Chapter 4. Other interviewees referred to the inclusion of regional development as a goal of the previous and new NDP,[67] the development of the NSS[68] and the commitment to a more effective regional monitoring system under the new NDP[69] as signs of progress.

On the negative side, while acknowledging the progress that had been achieved during the 'Celtic Tiger' period, several interviewees referred to the persistence of disparities and the non-delivery of stated policy goals as evidence that the policy had not been effective; for example, a central government interviewee[70] stated that 'good things have happened but not in the balanced way that we wanted'. Several references were made to some regions not doing particularly well,[71] and to missed opportunities due to the slow implementation of the NSS.[72] Regional policy was portrayed as having achieved some momentum in recent years, but it had not yet had a major impact:[73]

> In terms of momentum, the current policy has been quite effective, perhaps seven or eight out of ten. In terms of impact, I would say it has not yet reached its optimum.

One social partner interviewee[74] cited the huge investment that had taken place in recent years and the surge in population, particularly in the Mid-East region, without proper provision for sustainable transport and public amenities, as reasons to judge the policy as relatively ineffective. The NSS had come into play neither on time nor in an adequate way to prevent unsustainable settlement from taking place. A central government interviewee[75] stated that had the currently high investment in public infrastructure commenced sooner, the outcome would have been much better for the regions:

> I do think we will pay the price for that lack of accelerated investment in those particular areas and that more than anything else was the cause of why it wasn't as successful as it could have been in those particular regions.

67 Interviewee 21.
68 Interviewee 14.
69 Interviewee 5.
70 Interviewee 12.
71 Interviewee 17.
72 Interviewee 14.
73 Interviewee 2.
74 Interviewee 7.
75 Interviewee 12.

The conclusions that can be drawn from the responses to this question are that, viewed from the perspective of overall national prosperity, regional policy is seen as having been effective in recent years; but viewed from the perspective of reducing regional disparities, the response appeared to be contingent on what was considered by interviewees to be an acceptable level of regional disparities. The adequacy of the NSS process to prevent further unsustainable growth patterns was called into question.

The responses to this issue reflect the fact that the stated policy goal for regional policy has evolved from that stated in the previous NDP to that espoused in the NSS, and reinforced in the new NDP. Regional policy could be considered as ineffective in the recent past because the goal that then applied had not been achieved, in spite of the overall progress of the national economy. The variety of the responses also reflects the absence of a generally accepted metric to measure the success of regional policy. Were these in place and correctly applied, there could be no dispute about the extent to which regional policy had been effective.

The next phase of economic development may be more challenging and, if the attainment of regional balance is contingent on sustained investment and overall national growth, it may become extremely difficult to achieve continued growth in all regions, given a less benign global economy. In that context, the focusing of investment on the designated growth centres may be the most appropriate and coherent strategy.

Convergence and divergence forces

In the next question, interviewees were asked to identify what factors had given rise to the existing disparities and the forces they consider to be driving regional convergence and divergence in Ireland. This question is similar to a force-field analysis, a commonly used decision-making technique to identify and focus on strategies that accentuate favourable forces and mitigate the effects of negative forces. An understanding of the nature and scale of these forces is important in order to determine whether the current policy is sufficiently attuned to the forces that are likely to determine the spatial distribution of economic activity in Ireland in the future.

The sectoral composition of the regional economy was given as the primary cause of disparities by several interviewees, due to a high reliance on low-value sectors for employment in some regions. For example, according to one academic interviewee, 'the main differential in the productivity indices is due to the sectoral composition of the economy'.[76] Generations of out-migration had weakened the entrepreneurial capacity of

76 Interviewee 20.

some regions according to one regional interviewee.[77] The existing disparities were also attributed to the location decisions of large multinationals based in Ireland, attracted by access to the EU market, a low corporation tax rate and an English-speaking, educated workforce.[78] This broadly accords with the analysis of O'Leary (2002, 2007) and Morgenroth (2006). Differences in geography, natural endowments, the concentration of administrative power in Dublin and the legacy of under-investment in the western regions were further reasons given for the existence of disparities.[79] The Dublin region was described as an 'international gateway', attracting a high level of economic activity, by several interviewees.[80] The recent pattern of major infrastructure investment was viewed by a regional interviewee[81] as reinforcing the economic dominance of the Greater Dublin Area and 'sucking in' development from other regions.

It was predicted that global forces, movements in foreign direct investment and concentration of high-tech industries in a limited number of locations would drive further divergence.[82] Science, technology and innovation capacity were also viewed as forces for concentration of economic activity, particularly in the vicinity of the larger higher education institutions.[83] Regions currently reliant on traditional low-value sectors and construction-generated employment were viewed as being vulnerable to economic decline.[84] An academic interviewee[85] highlighted the limits to which regional policy can be effective in addressing the cumulative effects of the agglomeration economies at work:

> I think that one also has to accept that there are limits to regional policy. You will not make Leitrim as prosperous as Dublin no matter what you do because it doesn't have the density of population to support it.

The forces favouring greater regional balance were identified as the desire for a better quality of life and environment, reflecting a broader, less economistic view of development, as well as the greater use of distance-working facilitated by ICT and enhanced accessibility arising from the availability of improved transport links. For example, a regional interviewee[86] stated that:

77 Interviewee 9.
78 Interviewee 20.
79 Interviewees 4 and 9.
80 Interviewees 1, 18 and 22.
81 Interviewee 4.
82 Interviewee 22.
83 Interviewee 14.
84 Interviewees 9 and 14.
85 Interviewee 24.
86 Interviewee 11.

> If they [multinational companies] want to attract people they know that these people want to be somewhere they can send their kids to university and play golf and go sailing in their spare time. So I think that all of these things in terms of making a place attractive to live and work are part of the formula.

Regional investment, particularly in access infrastructure[87] and higher education participation,[88] was viewed as favouring convergence somewhat. In the event that the critical mass around the gateways and hubs is significantly increased, this could lead to greater convergence in regional economic performance.[89] Improved collaboration at regional level[90] and the recently increased valorisation of some land-based commodities[91] were seen as potential sources of convergence. Finally, EU receipts were perceived as having been supportive of convergence in the past, but would not be as relevant in the future.[92]

Overall, a majority of interviewees felt that the forces favouring economic concentration and wider disparities would predominate in the coming years. This would suggest that unless regional locations attain similar endowments as the existing cities that are performing well, they will not be competitive locations for further investment. The effectiveness of regional policy as it currently applies, in the face of these potentially strengthening forces, has to be called into question. Without targeted investment to enhance the productive capacity of all regions in a planned, coherent and integrated manner, the economic disparities between regions are likely to become exacerbated.

Preferred goals and influential policy drivers

Interviewees were asked what the overarching goal of regional policy should be in Ireland, and three alternatives were proffered to them. These were: cohesion, described as convergence in the economic performance of all regions; competitiveness, raising productivity and employment levels; and polycentric development, described as more balanced spatial structuring. It was suggested that the three alternative influential concepts implied quite distinctive spatial investment strategies and it was acknowledged that these alternatives were not mutually exclusive. The

87 Interviewees 15, 17 and 22.
88 Interviewees 18 and 19.
89 Interviewees 11 and 17.
90 Interviewee 12.
91 Interviewee 14.
92 Interviewee 24.

purpose of this question, which shifted the interview from a descriptive and evaluative to a normative format, was to determine the views of the four categories of interviewees on what the goal of regional policy should be, with particular reference to three alternative policy drivers.

Competitiveness was the preferred goal of more than half of the interviewees (13 out of 24) and at least one from each category supported this. It was suggested that wealth creation, prosperity and the wellbeing of the nation as a whole should be the aim and that these should take precedence over specific regional goals. An academic interviewee[93] defined the preferred goal in the following terms:

> Regions achieving their economic potential, potential now defined in terms of the maximum possible wellbeing of the citizens residing in those areas where that might involve growing divergence because the potential of one region happens to be higher than that of another.

Regional competitiveness, built around a coalition of regional and local interests, was identified as a contributor to national competitiveness and creating an environment or an 'ecosystem' favourable to business competitiveness. It was mentioned a number of times.[94]

Polycentric development was the second most popular overarching goal, identified by one-third of interviewees (8 out of 24); for example, a central government interviewee[95] stated that:

> Certainly, the last one, polycentric development, there is definitely a consciousness of the importance of that and unless you have a regional policy if you don't have an effective spatial framework or policy there, the whole thing will develop in an unsustainable way environmentally and economically.

It was anticipated that focusing on the attractiveness of the designated growth centres would have a lasting impact,[96] and a central government interviewee[97] stated that 'the planning system is in a very strong role to facilitate and manage growth and can influence decision-making across different sectors'. Contrary to this assertion, an academic interviewee[98] questioned the rationale of polycentric urban structuring as a policy goal, stating that it was poorly founded. A regional interviewee[99] described the

93 Interviewee 20.
94 Interviewees 6, 11 and 12.
95 Interviewee 1.
96 Interviewees 11, 22 and 24.
97 Interviewee 18.
98 Interviewee 23.
99 Interviewee 17.

role of effective spatial planning as 'overstated' and that this was not a driver of balanced economic growth:

> In terms of spatial planning it can be overstated in its role. At the end of the day the market will only invest in places that are competitive. Spatial planning can do a certain amount in indicating where enterprises can be located etc., but at the end of the day if an enterprise wanted to set up somewhere in Ireland, will spatial planning inhibit them?

These critiques reflect those of Parr (2005a), who questioned the superior economic performance attributed to polycentric urban development and suggested it should be considered as a guiding framework and not a regional policy in itself.

Cohesion was advocated by five interviewees as a means of ensuring equality of opportunity and access to services, and to avoid excessive disparities. A regional interviewee[100] suggested that a more rational approach to service provision was required, and that the levels of service available at appropriate spatial scales should be fully thought through. Cohesion as a goal was challenged by a central government interviewee[101] on the basis that a drive towards convergence might hold back the stronger regions:

> If you were to set yourself that [cohesion] as an objective, you run the danger if a particular region is doing well at a particular time that you should slow it down so it doesn't get ahead of the rest.

Some interviewees stated that none of the overarching goals should predominate, and there were suggestions of combinations of complementary goals. Several interviewees posited that enhanced productivity and employment growth in the context of proper spatial planning would attain a degree of convergence, effectively combining all three, reflecting the discussion on reconciling the concepts in an Irish context in Chapter 2. A central government interviewee[102] expressed it as follows:

> how our competitiveness and how our restructuring is happening will help to cohere and converge the various regions throughout the country. So that would be my order, that competitiveness would inform and drive polycentric development which would then in turn provide the sound basis for cohesion.

100 Interviewee 9.
101 Interviewee 1.
102 Interviewee 18.

Quality of life and sustainability were mentioned by a number of interviewees[103] as additional goals that should be taken into account, and a social partner interviewee[104] suggested that Ireland cannot compete with the economic giants in the long term and should valorise its natural assets and quality of life potential instead.

Although competitiveness was the preferred predominant goal of the interviewees, complementarity with other goals was frequently mentioned; for example, an academic interviewee[105] stated: 'so I think competitiveness remains and has to be very important and linked to that polycentric development'. As overall national competitiveness cannot be attained without having dynamic competitive regional locations (Gardiner et al., 2004), this suggests that a far greater focus is now needed on regional competitiveness in public policy, and that delivery of more effective spatial structuring is also required. In the context of a competitiveness-driven policy framework, the question remains as to what level of service should be available to all areas and what tolerance there should be for wider disparities in economic activity, should these arise. The goal suggested by a majority of interviewees is a measure of regional and national development, but does not capture balance.

Measurement

Interviewees were asked to suggest the criteria by which the success of regional policy should be measured. In any policy domain, having widely adopted performance indicators enables progress to be monitored, and these can serve as diagnostic indicators if desired outcomes are not being achieved. It is also important that appropriate arrangements be put in place to regularly collate, analyse and publish data to support monitoring.

The most commonly used indicator internationally has been GDP per capita or GVA, a related measure. This measure, for example, has been the key criterion to determine eligibility for higher rates of EU structural funds. However, as outlined in Chapter 2, it is considered to be a potentially misleading and narrow measure of true regional wellbeing in Ireland, due to its distortion by the transfer pricing engaged in by multinational corporations based in Ireland and its excessively economistic character.

Several interviewees referred to the limitations of GDP, citing its distorting effect in an Irish context; for example, an academic interviewee[106] described it as a 'meaningless measure of living standards' and a regional

103 Interviewees 5 and 22.
104 Interviewee 5.
105 Interviewee 24.
106 Interviewee 20.

interviewee[107] stated that GDP is 'one of the worst possible measures they could take in relation to economic wellbeing, particularly in the Irish case'. Many[108] stated that due to the complexity of regional policy issues, there was no single ideal measure that could be adopted as the benchmark of progress, unlike for example the long-term unemployment rate as a key measure of labour market policy. Specific indicators mentioned included measures of income, employment, regional output, innovation capacity, social deprivation levels, higher education participation, sectoral structure and quality of services.

One academic interviewee[109] stated that all public policies should be amenable to measurement:

> All public policies need to be measured, evaluated, analysed and adapted as part of the public policy process, and yes, you should have indicators but what those indicators should be is a difficult question.

Two interviewees[110] suggested that ongoing monitoring of overall context indicators such as regional GDP, disposable incomes and employment creation should be combined with specific performance indicators for individual programmes and benchmarks for the provision of services at appropriate spatial scales. A comprehensive regional data system is to be established by the Spatial Policy Unit in the Department of the Environment, Heritage and Local Government, linked with the NSS monitoring system.

Two interviewees[111] mentioned the limitations of having 'potential' as the national goal for regional policy, as this is perceived as an amorphous concept that is not fixed in time, echoing the concerns expressed by Morgenroth (2003a). Regional income measures based on place of residence were seen as being influenced by unsustainable inter-regional commuting, giving a potentially misleading indication of balanced development.[112]

Two interviewees[113] identified quality of life as an indicator that should be measured regionally, using an appropriately constructed index that reflects what matters to people; for example, an academic interviewee[114] stated that:

---

107 Interviewee 11.

108 Interviewees 14, 21 and 23.

109 Interviewee 19.

110 Interviewees 6 and 9.

111 Interviewees 1 and 23

112 Interviewees 18 and 21.

113 Interviewees 20 and 22.

114 Interviewee 22.

> There are lots of indices of the quality of life around combining income and other measures such as the human development index developed by the UN, and I think they would show that things are much more equal between the regions than the more income-based ones that we seem to focus on quite a lot.

The two regional assemblies in conjunction with the Spatial Policy Unit commissioned the construction of a gateway development index for the designated gateways, involving both objective and subjective measures. This was published in 2009.

A social partner interviewee[115] stated that there was too much emphasis in the public sector on measuring inputs and not enough on measuring outputs. There was no reference by interviewees to the use of secondary aggregative indicators such as coefficient of variation (e.g. σ-convergence) to capture the level of dispersal of primary data such as regional GVA, disposable income and employment.

Overall, the six indicators chosen to demonstrate recent regional socioeconomic trends in Chapter 4 broadly reflect the views of interviewees on the key measures of regional socioeconomic development. The lack of a widely accepted measure of the performance of regional policy hinders objective assessments of its success or otherwise. Neither the current goal of regional policy – as perceived by most interviewees – nor the preferred goal proffered by most interviewees is amenable to a simple measure of success. It is too early to assess the quality of the regional data monitoring system currently being developed by the Spatial Policy Unit.

In the context of measuring competitiveness, an annual benchmarking of Ireland's competitiveness performance is carried out based on a pyramid model devised and applied by the National Competitiveness Council, operating under the auspices of Forfás. The regional competitiveness model developed by Cambridge Econometrics, which customises understandings of the inputs and intermediary outputs to the regional level, as referred to in Chapter 2, would provide a useful framework within which to benchmark regional competitiveness.

Investment planning and investment strategies

Investment planning, spatial planning and governance arrangements are the three key dimensions of regional policy in Ireland that are the subjects of this study. The question on investment planning related to both the process by which investments are prioritised and the content of the investment

115 Interviewee 6.

strategies. The responses to these issues are considered separately in the following subsections.

Investment planning process

The process of identifying and prioritising public investment is an important dimension of territorial governance. Several interviewees[116] stated that investment planning in Ireland is excessively sector-driven and not sufficiently spatially driven and that a more territorially focused process is needed; for example, a regional interviewee[117] stated:

> The system itself would tend to work against regional policy at the national level. The system tends to focus on the functional areas of transport and communications – departmental thinking.

An academic interviewee[118] attributed this to the centralised nature of Irish public administration and the fact that civil servants are more attuned to sectoral programming:

> They work within a particular model or paradigm of how investments are made whereas the kind of thinking that the DoE [Department of the Environment] is trying to bring to this is more lateral thinking and this is not widespread across the other departments.

The co-ordination of public policy delivery across sectoral domains at regional and local levels was described as weak.[119] A central government interviewee[120] acknowledged that horizontal co-ordination at regional level is deficient, but stated that shifting from vertical to horizontal accountability would require a radical overhaul of public administration and that incremental rather than radical change would be preferable. The NSS was identified[121] as a potential catalyst for better engagement between national agencies and regional bodies and to co-ordinate land-use, transport and other investments, although there was only limited evidence, according to two regional interviewees,[122] that this was currently taking place. A regional interviewee[123] stated:

---

116 Interviewees 3, 4, 14, 17 and 22.
117 Interviewee 3.
118 Interviewee 21.
119 Interviewees 12 and 22.
120 Interviewee 15.
121 Interviewee 10.
122 Interviewees 13 and 14.
123 Interviewee 13.

> I would like to see a clearer focus in government investment decision-making on gateways and hubs … it's not clear to me that there have been any changes in the scoring system or the assessment system which gives any more weighting to a proposal from a hub or gateway.

Asymmetric approaches were advocated by a central government interviewee[124] to take account of uneven development potential and to enable regions to respond flexibly to their own identified priorities. The current department-led system, according to several interviewees, is designed to protect departmental patches,[125] is excessively top-down[126] and is leading to a segmented, poorly integrated approach regionally;[127] another viewed the NDP planning system as too high-level to reflect specific regional priorities.[128]

A central government interviewee[129] stated that sectoral interaction takes place regionally and that it is at this level that spatial integration is best achieved. An enhancement of the role of local authorities in co-ordinating the availability of public services was suggested by two regional interviewees.[130] It was suggested by an academic interviewee[131] that all national policies should be spatially proofed to avoid the negative regional consequences of spatially blind 'one size fits all' approaches:

> that all policies would be spatially proofed; that someone would look at them from a spatial point of view before they are finalised, which is not happening.

This could involve territorial impact analysis, on an interdepartmental basis, of the investment plans of national agencies and semi-state bodies, guided by overall regional policy goals and obliging departments and agencies to have regional as well as national strategies.

A more rigorous prior appraisal of investment needs and of large-scale projects at national and regional levels was advocated, amid claims that some investment proposals put forward in the past had lacked realism.[132] It was suggested[133] that the capacity and comparative advantages of each region should be more rigorously assessed to demonstrate the added value

124 Interviewee 2.
125 Interviewee 8.
126 Interviewee 17.
127 Interviewee 3.
128 Interviewee 4.
129 Interviewee 12.
130 Interviewees 9 and 13.
131 Interviewee 22.
132 Interviewee 11.
133 Interviewee 2.

and contribution of proposed investments to overall national output. The current cost–benefit analysis approach to project appraisal was described as too narrow by two interviewees[134] (one academic and one central government), as it failed to capture and monetise all the spatial implications. One central government interviewee[135] identified the role of government as reconciling competing demands in the context of limited public resources: 'there is at national level a sense of priority about what needs to be done but there's never going to be enough money to do everything'. Across the four categories of interviewees, regional bodies tended to be most critical of the strategic investment planning process as it currently operates. Central government and agency interviewees were least critical of the investment planning process.

The process by which the NDP is prepared would appear to be coherent from the perspective of central government. It draws together the multiannual spending plans of all departments and integrates national strategies such as the transport strategy (Transport 21), the National Anti-Poverty Strategy and the Strategy for Science, Technology and Innovation into the government's own spending framework. However, the coherence of this process at regional level was questioned by several interviewees. The investment priorities put forward at regional level are not incorporated effectively in national plans or implemented as integrated regional investment strategies, and the regional impacts of national programmes are not assessed in any structured way. The capacity at regional level to identify, evaluate, prioritise and sequence alternative investment proposals was identified as weak.

Content of investment strategies

There is a strong link between the type and location of public investment and the outcomes in terms of the spatial distribution of productive capacity and income levels. Investment in transport infrastructure was mentioned most frequently as accessibility and connectivity, particularly to the designated growth centres, were considered to be conducive to driving regional competitiveness; for example, a central government interviewee[136] stated that 'I think that you need your transport infrastructure in place before you attract your firms or investors'. The need for compact connected urban spaces with rapid public transport links to facilitate more sustainable settlement was also highlighted,[137] and conventional roads-led investment

134 Interviewees 10 and 23.
135 Interviewee 1.
136 Interviewee 10.
137 Interviewee 6.

strategies were criticised by some interviewees for their lack of foresight.[138]

Two interviewees (one academic,[139] one social partner[140]) expressed concern that prioritising the construction of the radial motorway network from Dublin had extended its commuting radius, and that transport can 'suck the factors of production out of the nearby regions', thus contributing to urban sprawl. This supports the assertion of Dall'erba and Le Gallo (2003) that investment in hub-and-spoke interconnections does not necessarily benefit the region where they are implemented. On the other hand, two central government interviewees[141] stated that this investment had greatly facilitated inward investment into Ireland, with one[142] describing the inter-urban routes as 'a precondition for regional development in Ireland'. Broadband services were identified by four interviewees[143] as essential to enable businesses across Ireland to operate effectively, wherever they are located.

Creating a suitable environment to facilitate indigenous enterprise was also highlighted by five interviewees,[144] citing the likely decline in Ireland's future share of FDI as a reason for this. For example, a central government interviewee[145] stated that 'the development of the indigenous sector is absolutely critical and in developing the indigenous sector we want to develop the whole area of entrepreneurship'. This should be considered in the context of Bradley's assertion (2002) that the capacity of regions in Ireland to influence the economic environment in which enterprises operate is somewhat restricted.

It was stated that knowledge-based production had been largely tied up in inward investment and that there was now a need to build a regional research and innovation support base to counter the low R&D activity levels among indigenous firms; for example, a central government interviewee[146] stated:

> the future development of Ireland will depend on its science knowledge base for the economy and society, rather than the older version of production and output ... we need to have our economic activity driven by knowledge and in order to get there we need to do more research and development and innovation.

---

138 Interviewee 14.
139 Interviewee 21.
140 Interviewee 6.
141 Interviewees 10 and 15.
142 Interviewee 15.
143 Interviewees 14, 17, 18 and 24.
144 Interviewees 4, 12, 15, 16 and 20.
145 Interviewee 12.
146 Interviewee 16.

However, an academic interviewee[147] acknowledged that there was some resistance at national level to considering science policy at regional level. An enhanced role for higher education institutions was advocated by three interviewees,[148] with stronger links to regional economic development strategies. Two interviewees[149] referred to the reorganisation of the health service and said that a more rational provision of services at regional level was needed. The same two interviewees cited investment in tourism as a stimulant of economic activity in underdeveloped regions.

The investment strategies identified by the interviewees largely reflect those in the NDP relating to transport, the productive sector and social infrastructure. The differential spatial impacts of the chosen investment strategies, and the fact that many of these strategies lack spatial considerations and that no co-ordinated regional innovation strategies are in place, were raised by some interviewees.

Spatial planning

The purpose of this question was to determine the views of the interviewees on the application of spatial planning in Ireland. The primary spatial planning framework is the National Spatial Strategy (NSS), adopted in 2002; seven[150] Regional Planning Guidelines were adopted by the regional authorities in 2004. Most individual planning decisions in Ireland are taken by local authorities, in accordance with the relevant County Development Plan, which must have regard to the Regional Planning Guidelines.

In response to this question, there was widespread support for the concept of having a spatial strategy and the objectives of the NSS were generally endorsed by the interviewees; for example, an academic interviewee[151] stated that:

> the NSS is the main framework for that [regional policy] and I think the city regions model is the right way to go in that regard. It means ensuring that the major urban centres and their hinterlands are operating in an effective fashion and those are suitably spread around the country.

Spatial planning was said to be an essential basis for regional policy and the NSS was described as the 'most sustained regional policy effort' by one

---

147 Interviewee 22.
148 Interviewees 3, 6 and 7.
149 Interviewees 5 and 9.
150 The Regional Planning Guidelines for Dublin and the Mid-East NUTS III regions were combined.
151 Interviewee 22.

regional interviewee.[152] Several central government interviewees expressed confidence that the NSS would be successful in managing future economic development, provided that it is effectively translated into regional and local land-use strategies and into sectoral strategies; for example, a central government interviewee[153] stated that:

> In terms of sustainable land-use, one of the core pillars of the NSS is to ensure joined-up and linked policies between the national, regional and local levels to ensure that any future land use and transport plans are interlinked to ensure that you don't contribute to the urban sprawl that has happened in various parts of the country.

Other interviewees were more circumspect about the capacity of the NSS to enable a counterbalance to the Greater Dublin Area to be developed. Several interviewees[154] opined that too many gateways and hubs were designated under the spatial strategy and that some of the growth centres selected, especially the hubs, lacked the critical mass to drive the growth of their hinterlands or to compete internationally. Some suggested that the growth centres should have been limited to those identified in the NDP 2000–06, i.e. the regional cities, and that investment should be focused on enhancing their attractiveness and linking them to their hinterlands. One social partner interviewee[155] stated that the government is 'struggling to find a way of doing those gateways, of doing that number'.

A regional interviewee[156] suggested that a greater focus be put on the 'new' gateways, particularly in the North-West in order to strengthen the economy of that region. It was acknowledged that although the NSS had been grounded in detailed spatial analysis,[157] it had involved some political compromises; some interviewees considered that an NSS with a smaller number of gateways and hubs would not have garnered sufficient political support. An academic interviewee[158] stated that:

> I think what we've got was a political outcome that if one had pushed for greater precision and to leave some places out altogether and to have fewer of them, we would probably never have got an NSS.

---

152 Interviewee 13.
153 Interviewee 18.
154 Interviewees 5, 7 and 20.
155 Interviewee 6.
156 Interviewee 9.
157 Interviewee 9.
158 Interviewee 21.

Several interviewees raised the need for greater discipline in the enforcement of planning guidelines,[159] requiring a strengthening of the role of the regional authorities to ensure that the local area plans of local authorities and the sectoral strategies of government agencies complied with the Regional Planning Guidelines. One academic interviewee[160] stated that the local planning system is only 'theoretically linked with the Regional Planning Guidelines, which are more than theoretically linked to the National Spatial Strategy', i.e. that individual planning decisions do not always reflect the spirit of the planning guidelines. This is consistent with the recommendations of Fitzpatrick Associates et al. (2006) regarding the necessity for investment prioritisation and policy co-ordination in order to ensure the effective implementation of the NSS.

A number of interviewees[161] raised the lack of visible progress in implementing the NSS; it was stated that the expected increased investment in the gateways had not materialised and that the objective of providing a counterbalance to the growth of the Greater Dublin Area, in terms of population and economic activity, had not yet been achieved.[162] From a central government perspective,[163] it was stated that the failure of some gateways to progress reflected their inability to present their case coherently:

> There are some who are more proactive in lobbying their case, their needs, their claims, making a case for their weaknesses, the challenges that they face and coming up with coherent, with innovative solutions for that.

The fact that the functional areas of several gateways transcended local administrative boundaries was also cited[164] as a challenge to be overcome, suggesting that single gateway authorities may be a more effective mechanism. The Gateway Innovation Fund was cited as a positive development,[165] although one interviewee considered the scale of additional funds available to be too small to effect any significant change. The government's commitment to the NSS was called into question by a regional interviewee[166] in the context of a reduction in the budgetary allocation to the Gateway Innovation Fund:

---

159 Interviewees 1, 7, 14 and 17.
160 Interviewee 19.
161 Interviewees 5, 9, 13 and 17.
162 Interviewee 17.
163 Interviewee 1.
164 Interviewee 20.
165 Interviewees 3 and 22.
166 Interviewee 14.

> one sees in the recent announcement of savings by government that the gateway investment fund is one of the first areas targeted. I would have thought if they were serious about the National Spatial Strategy that that investment would have remained in place as an important contributor towards regional development, but as it has been targeted immediately, it goes to show that government pays lip service to regional policy.

Two regional interviewees questioned the real standing of the NSS across government departments,[167] echoing NESC's (2005) view in relation to the challenge of ensuring that the NSS is embedded in public investment decisions. One social partner interviewee[168] suggested that Ireland risked 'falling between stools' with too many inadequately developed gateways and an inefficient Dublin region. The insufficient number of staff employed in the Spatial Policy Unit,[169] the lack of clear targets in the NSS[170] and the delay in getting the NSS monitoring framework in place[171] were also identified as deficiencies. The failure of the government's decentralisation programme to align itself with the NSS was cited by a social partner interviewee[172] as evidence of a lack of real commitment to or understanding of the need for focused and enhanced investment in the designated growth centres, rather than a 'something for everyone' approach, stating that 'it broke everything that they said in the spatial strategy'.

Three interviewees[173] stated that the NSS had not taken sufficient cognisance of the spatial implications of the strengthening of the Dublin–Belfast corridor; for example, an academic interviewee[174] said that:

> the traditional dominance of the Dublin metropolitan region is changing to a very strong corridor now running from Belfast down along the east coast and I don't think that we have woken up to the dynamics of that. There's such a concentration now of population and economic activity in that line along the east coast that it has consequences for cities like Cork, Limerick and Galway.

Some interviewees[175] stressed the need for the development of the Atlantic

167 Interviewees 9 and 14.
168 Interviewee 6.
169 Interviewee 9.
170 Interviewee 7.
171 Interviewee 18.
172 Interviewee 8.
173 Interviewees 3, 7 and 24.
174 Interviewee 24.
175 Interviewees 11, 14, 17 and 18.

corridor to rival the dominance of the burgeoning Dublin–Belfast corridor. Corridor strategies were described as a natural progression of the gateway strategy, providing a greater level of regional agglomeration. For example, a regional interviewee[176] stated:

> The likes of the Atlantic Gateway corridor, if that is implemented as a corridor along the west of Ireland, is promoted and developed then it can provide a counterbalance to Dublin and the east coast economic corridor.

However, the likelihood of the Atlantic Corridor having a major impact was questioned by two interviewees.[177] Others[178] suggested that the spatial encroachment of Dublin on other regions should be better managed. It was also stated[179] that the extent of urban sprawl and unsustainable dormitory commuting had increased greatly in recent years. The lack of an emphasis on provincial towns and smaller centres of population was raised by some regional interviewees.[180] It was suggested[181] that such centres should focus on their quality-of-life offering and that investment should improve linkages to the main growth centres to avoid these towns becoming even more marginalised.

Although the NSS has largely defined the regional policy agenda in Ireland over the past six years, many view it as ineffective in achieving its stated goals. A review of the NSS may be warranted on the grounds that all the selected gateways and hubs cannot achieve the critical mass needed to drive regional economic growth. A more effective planning enforcement regime is also required in order to manage the growth of the Greater Dublin Area and to facilitate the acceleration of the development of the gateways and hubs. A perception, particularly at regional level, that the gateways have not received the investment they need has served to underline a perceived lack of commitment by central government to the NSS.

Territorial governance

Determining the appropriate territorial level for the identification and resolution of regional economic problems and improving territorial governance, through mechanisms of horizontal and vertical co-ordination

176 Interviewee 17.
177 Interviewees 11 and 14.
178 Interviewees 21 and 24.
179 Interviewees 21 and 22.
180 Interviewees 3 and 9.
181 Interviewee 17.

and devolution of authority, were identified in Chapter 2 as important mechanisms of regional policy. Similarly, the potential for national policy to have an enhanced territorialised dimension was highlighted as an important regional policy approach. Interviewees were asked for their perspectives on territorial governance in Ireland and to identify what organisations should be responsible for drawing up, implementing and evaluating investment plans and spatial frameworks. This question is linked to an earlier question on investment planning and also to the final question on the role of regional bodies in Ireland.

Several interviewees[182] stressed the highly centralised culture of Irish public administration and acknowledged that territorial governance arrangements are inadequate. The need for greater economic and fiscal responsibility to be devolved to subnational level was highlighted by many interviewees.[183] For example, an academic interviewee[184] stated that:

> We have an incredibly centralised system of government. We may have lots of local authorities and we do have assemblies and regional authorities, but the actual decision-making at the end of the day for practically everything gets to be made centrally.

A strengthened regional tier, it was suggested,[185] would enable the effective co-production of public policies and provide a mechanism to tailor national policies to regional needs, as proposed by Parr (2001). Centralised governance and the low level of localised taxation, according to one academic interviewee,[186] had created a dependency mentality; another[187] cited a lack of economic maturity at subnational level.

Several interviewees[188] identified the absence of a central government unit with responsibility for the co-ordination of regional policy as a key issue. For example, a regional interviewee stated:

> I don't see any co-ordinated or coherent evaluation of regional policy or approaches. I would see a fairly strong incoherence. This is probably the result of there being no government department with responsibility for regional policy: OK, the DoE [Department of the Environment] has responsibility for the NSS, but regional policy doesn't feature in central government thinking and it's not led by a lead department.

182 Interviewees 4, 5, 13, 21 and 23.
183 Interviewees 13, 15, 20 and 23.
184 Interviewee 20.
185 Interviewees 4, 15, 19, 20 and 24.
186 Interviewee 21.
187 Interviewee 20.
188 Interviewees 1, 2, 5, 14 and 17.

An enhanced role for the Spatial Policy Unit (SPU), with a greater breadth of expertise, e.g. in spatial economics and spatial investment analysis, was proposed by several interviewees.[189] The level of spatial expertise in the SPU and existing linkages with government departments were cited in support of this. For example, a central government interviewee[190] stated that:

> the NSS people in the Department of the Environment have got involved in and they have taken the lead in a lot of areas of drawing together the different players. They have a group where the government departments are brought together to see how different sectoral policies should march in alignment.

Two interviewees[191] recommended an expanded remit for the Department of Community, Rural and Gaeltacht Affairs; two[192] suggested that the remit for regional policy co-ordination should be housed within the Department of Finance; and a further two[193] suggested the Department of the Taoiseach, for this enhanced role.

The limited political support for a strengthened regional tier from either central or local government was identified,[194] and one academic interviewee[195] stated that:

> The strength of the county in Ireland is as important to the dynamic as the level of centralisation. I can't see it. I can't see any political forces that want it. The danger is that it would become another tier which increases the transaction cost.

Overcoming clientelism and localism in the Irish political culture was highlighted[196] as a challenge. The quality of interaction between central and regional level was identified as a problem.[197] A model of increased policy co-production, as practised in The Netherlands, was advocated by two interviewees – one academic[198] and one social partner.[199] A system of

189 Interviewees 2, 17, 18 and 22.
190 Interviewee 1.
191 Interviewees 4 and 5.
192 Interviewees 8 and 19.
193 Interviewees 12 and 14.
194 Interviewees 14, 17 and 24.
195 Interviewee 24.
196 Interviewee 24.
197 Interviewee 19.
198 Interviewee 19.
199 Interviewee 5.

networked governance with multilevel, multi-party engagement around key initiatives was also advocated by two interviewees.[200]

Two interviewees[201] criticised enterprise agencies for being answerable to their national authorities only and not obliged to dovetail their plans with those of the regional authorities. One regional interviewee[202] suggested that central government should direct national agencies to fulfil their regional policy obligations; an academic interviewee[203] stated it as follows:

> What's missing at the county level and also at the regional level is that there is no onus on those agencies to dovetail with what is going on. They are involved on the county development boards but they don't have to answer to them or show how they have taken cognisance of the strategies that they have agreed. Unless you build that in at region level, the co-ordination isn't going to work.

Subnational co-ordinating bodies such as regional authorities and county development boards (within local authorities) were described[204] as leading 'precarious existences' without adequate resources or powers. An enhanced strategic policy analysis capacity, increased co-ordination across sectoral programmes and a strengthened ability to prioritise investment proposals in order to drive the regional policy agenda were advocated by several interviewees.[205] This would accord with the ideal of region-level planning of investment, within a supportive national framework, suggested by Morgan (2002). A central government interviewee[206] identified the higher education institutions as an untapped source of strategic regional policy intelligence.

Two interviewees[207] felt that a process of regional proofing was needed and that sectoral programmes should have explicit spatial goals in order to bring regional policy more centrally into national policymaking; for example, an academic interviewee[208] recommended:

> That all policies would be spatially proofed, that someone would look at them from a spatial point of view before they are finalised, which is not happening I don't think.

200 Interviewees 6 and 18.
201 Interviewees 4 and 19.
202 Interviewee 4.
203 Interviewee 19.
204 Interviewee 6.
205 Interviewees 2, 9 and 19.
206 Interviewee 1.
207 Interviewees 22 and 23.
208 Interviewee 22.

However, the Irish experience of policy proofing was described as 'disappointing' by one of the social partner interviewees.[209]

A social partner interviewee[210] viewed local government as a form of local administration of national policy and as being excessively dependent on central government, with insufficient fiscal autonomy. Two academic interviewees[211] proposed that responsibility for the delivery of public goods should be allocated across different tiers of government according to administrative efficiency criteria and that tax-raising powers should be aligned with this.

This assessment of territorial governance in Ireland adheres to O'Hara and Commins's (2003) depiction of 'functional regionalism' in which regional policies are determined centrally to be administered regionally, but with little or no regional differentiation. These findings suggest that there is a need for a unit within government to be assigned responsibility for the co-ordination of regional policy and to introduce procedures across government to ensure that territorial objectives are more coherently integrated into public policy. Mechanisms to engage regional economic actors were considered by Keating (1997) to be a prerequisite for effective regional economic development. A policy co-production approach would require that regional and local tiers acquire the necessary strategic capability, resources and authority to enable them to engage more constructively with central government authorities and agencies.

Role of regional bodies

The final question on the interview guide related to the specific roles that interviewees considered should be played by region-level bodies; interviewees were also asked what additional powers, if any, should be devolved to them. The literature on devolution and economic governance that was reviewed in Chapter 2 pointed to the establishment of stronger regional institutions as contributors to enhanced institutional capacity, democratic engagement, political leadership and consensus-building, as well as to accountability and administrative efficiency.

It was almost unanimously accepted that the existing regional bodies lacked significant powers, a point also made in the Green Paper on Local Government (DEHLG, 2008). An academic interview[212] stated the position as follows:

---

209 Interviewee 6.

210 Interviewee 8.

211 Interviewees 20 and 23.

212 Interviewee 19.

> Going back to the structures and the funding at regional level they have always been functionally limited and financially constricted and that goes back to what I was saying about no conversion to regionalism on behalf of our government.

Several interviewees[213] suggested that the NUTS III level is closest to the most appropriate level for enhanced economic governance and that powers should be enhanced at this level to enable regional bodies to perform as both co-ordinating and deliberative arenas in relation to the setting of strategic direction, defining regional visions and the development of coherent regional investment packages. A central government interviewee[214] stated:

> We must develop comparative advantages for individual regions. National planning sometimes smoothes over regional differences. Regional bodies should have a greater role in directing and shaping.

A view of one central government interviewee[215] was that regional authorities were not adequately exercising their existing powers. Two academic interviewees[216] posited that some functions currently exercised by local authorities could be better exercised at regional authority level.

The differing conceptualisations of regions in Ireland and the stronger affinity to county identities have implications for regional governance and for defining the geographical boundaries of appropriate regional entities, according to some interviewees. One academic interviewee[217] stated that:

> there is no identification of the public with regions either and there doesn't seem to be any desire for that. If you ask people about the regional assembly or the regional authority, unless they are politically active most people won't have taken any notice of them.

Several interviewees[218] suggested that in order to attain greater coherence, there should be a reconfiguration of existing structures to create one tier of regional governance and that the number of regions should be less than eight (the current number of regional authorities) and greater than two (the number of regional assemblies). For example, a regional interviewee[219] stated that:

213 Interviewees 2, 7, 9, 10, 13, 15, 17, 21 and 22.
214 Interviewee 2.
215 Interviewee 1.
216 Interviewees 19 and 22.
217 Interviewee 19.
218 Interviewees 7, 9, 12, 13, 19, 20, 21 and 22.
219 Interviewee 9.

> I think that this level of governance needs to be reorganised and strengthened and be given a much clearer role and mandate in order to better address the needs of regions.

Some suggested[220] that four or five would be more reflective of the functional economic areas of the economy, with better transport linkages. Two interviewees[221] recommended that a single regional tier should incorporate not only the regional assemblies and authorities but also bodies such as the Western Development Commission, Shannon Development and Udarás na Gaeltachta and the regional offices of the enterprise agencies. One regional interviewee[222] suggested an amalgamation of all three subnational tiers into a single tier of regional governance, but acknowledged that this proposal was unlikely to gain political support.

Two central government interviewees[223] acknowledged that the regional bodies were under-utilised in public administration and that they could make a far greater contribution; for example, a central government interviewee[224] stated:

> I think they are being under-utilised at the moment … and they're in an ideal position to assess what is being delivered, what policies are working and I think that's where they have potential to add value to the process.

Two interviewees[225] suggested that there should be a direct engagement on an equal footing between regional bodies and national government bodies in undertaking spatial analysis and strategic planning, with an obligation to progress agreed priorities. For example, a regional interviewee[226] stated that:

> The role [of enhanced regional bodies] could include research and analysis, strategic planning and co-ordination with a requirement for central government to engage directly with this regional level in identifying and prioritising investments priorities.

This echoes the concept of policy co-production, advocated by an academic interviewee,[227] as referred to in an earlier section. The need to bring

220 Interviewees 7, 11, 12 and 19.
221 Interviewees 17 and 19.
222 Interviewee 11.
223 Interviewees 2 and 18.
224 Interviewee 18.
225 Interviewees 2 and 9.
226 Interviewee 9.
227 Interviewee 19.

policymaking closer to policy implementation was highlighted by a social partner interviewee.[228]

Regional policy as it related to the rationale, establishment and functions of the regional authorities and regional assemblies was described by one interviewee[229] as a 'contrived policy' and by another[230] as an 'artefact of EU policy', designed to satisfy EU demands for a greater regional input into programme planning and monitoring. The existing regional bodies' configuration was described as having limited clout and impact[231] and it was stated that there was a limited awareness of their role.[232] A regional interviewee[233] said that:

> We haven't a very good history of institutionalised regional policy. Regional authorities have very little power and influence and also Irish regions are too small. We have eight regions, and that is too many.

The limited powers of regional authority Directors *vis-à-vis* County Managers in respect of planning was identified by one academic interviewee[234] as a major issue.

A number of interviewees[235] considered the NUTS II regions to be heterogeneous and saw a limited long-term role for the regional assemblies if there is no EU regional funding distinction post-2013. A regional interviewee[236] stated that:

> The regional authorities were put in as a means of keeping Europe happy, the regional assemblies were put in as a means of hanging on to the cash and that game is over now I think. So I don't know what the role of the regional assemblies will be.

One regional interviewee[237] stated that the regional assemblies had established an expertise in the management of EU programmes that could be applied to other domains, and that the established linkages with EU regional institutions and networks were potentially very valuable for Irish regional policy.

---

228 Interviewee 6.
229 Interviewee 9.
230 Interviewee 20.
231 Interviewees 3, 9 and 23.
232 Interviewees 4 and 19.
233 Interviewee 3.
234 Interviewee 21.
235 Interviewees 4, 11, 13, 15, 17 and 20.
236 Interviewee 11.
237 Interviewee 14.

Some interviewees[238] recommended that regional bodies needed fiscal autonomy and a democratic mandate in order to be more effective; for example, a regional interviewee[239] stated:

> so I think the taxation and representation principle, there has to be something there. I think there should be responsibility for revenue-raising, there would be democratic accountability then.

The governance structures of both regional authorities and regional assemblies were criticised for having local authority members only. One regional interviewee[240] recommended professional practitioners on an executive-type board.

The establishment of regional structures as pragmatic responses to EU programming requirements and the limited functions and impact of the regional bodies were highlighted, echoing some of the literature reviewed in Chapter 2, e.g. Morgenroth (2000) and Laffan (2004). This is somewhat incongruous with the recognised role of the regional level as the arena for competitive advantage and the need for some degree of strategic autonomy at this level (Gardiner et al., 2004). Regional policy coherence and the attainment of the stated goals for regional policy in terms of maximising potential are unlikely to be attained without an enhanced role for region-level bodies. In the context of a weakening EU-derived rationale for regional structures, a functional rationale based on meeting national policy objectives, in particular the effective delivery of the NSS, now exists. This is echoed in the NESC prescription (2008) of a recasting of regional administration to support the development of the gateway regions. A further examination of the number of regional bodies and the coherence of the existing regional boundaries would appear to be warranted.

Chapter conclusions

This chapter set out and discussed the findings that derived from the semi-structured interviews with the four categories of interviewees. The need to develop the assets of all regions in order to maximise overall national efficiency was cited as the most common rationale, with equity and administrative efficiency arguments far less common. It was also suggested that regional differences provide a justification for regional policies that cohere spatially. The National Spatial Strategy has largely set the agenda in terms of defining the overarching goal for regional policy in Ireland. This

238 Interviewees 11, 13, 17, 20 and 24.

239 Interviewee 13.

240 Interviewee 4.

is consistent with the rationale but doesn't lend itself to precise measurement. The NSS was also identified as the most prominent feature of regional policy. Regional policy was generally considered as secondary to sectoral policy with limited evidence of policy differentiation, suggesting that a structured mechanism to ensure better horizontal co-ordination or 'territorialisation' of policies is required.

There were mixed views on the effectiveness of regional policy over the past decade, and the attribution of recent economic success to national rather than regional policy was considered a factor. An implication of this finding is that regional disparities are likely to increase in an economic downturn. Neither the current goal of regional policy, as perceived by a majority of interviewees, nor the preferred goal proffered is amenable to a simple measure of success. The absence of clear metrics renders it difficult to assess effectiveness objectively. Many of the interviewees predicted that the forces that drive greater economic concentration are likely to intensify and that targeted investment will be needed to enhance the productive capacity of all regions in a planned and coherent manner.

More than half of the interviewees considered that attaining competitiveness should be the overarching goal of Irish regional policy, implying that a far greater focus is required on regional competitiveness in public policy in view of the acknowledged regional foundations of national competitiveness. It was considered that the process of preparing the main investment strategic document, i.e. the NDP, was coherent from the perspective of meeting national programming requirements, but it was also considered that this document was excessively sector-driven and did not adequately meet the need for coherent regional investment strategies. Investment needs prioritised by interviewees were transport infrastructure, ICT, support for enterprises and commercialisation of research outputs. It was acknowledged that the differential regional requirements for these investments are not always reflected in the national investment plans.

There was wide support for the principal objectives of the NSS, but many viewed it as ineffective to date and as not fully embedded in public policies. The need for stricter planning enforcement, single gateway authorities and greater co-ordination of investments at gateway level was identified. Territorial governance arrangements in Ireland were generally viewed as weak, with the absence of a central department with responsibility for regional policy cited as a particular weakness. A new approach based on policy co-production was advocated by some interviewees, with a need for an enhanced policy analysis capacity within regional bodies. There was some support for a reconfiguration of the two tiers of regional administration into a single tier with an enhancement of the powers of regional administration to fulfil a strategic planning, prioritisation and co-ordination role, with the full co-operation of central government and its agencies.

Differences in responses were discernible across the four categories of interviewee. Interviewees from regional bodies tended to be more critical of the coherence of the investment planning processes, the effectiveness of regional policy and the likelihood of success of the NSS, whereas those from the national bodies tended to have a more benign view of these. There were also opposing views on the reasons for the slow progress in implementing the NSS, with the central government interviewees highlighting the failure of gateway authorities to operate coherently and those from regional bodies emphasising the lack of prioritisation of public investment. Central government and agency interviewees were quite consistent in defining the current regional policy goal as that set out in the NSS. Academic interviewees tended to view regional policy goals as aspirational political goals rather than as meaningful measurable objectives.

6

Summary, Conclusions and Recommendations

This chapter draws together conclusions on the substantive issues addressed in the study and the implications of these for Irish regional policy. It commences with a summary of the findings of the research as set out in Chapters 4 and 5, with reference to the relevant literature reviewed in Chapter 2.

From these findings, conclusions are drawn with respect to the overall research questions on the coherence of Irish regional policy. The implications of the findings and conclusions are then considered, in relation to investment planning, spatial planning and territorial governance in Ireland. Conclusions are also drawn on the utility of policy coherence as a policy analysis framework. Some recommendations arising from the conclusions are set out. Finally, the limitations of the research undertaken and some areas that merit further study are identified.

The key findings as summarised below are structured around the themes in the interview guide.

Summary of findings by theme

Rationale

Overall, the economic efficiency arguments in favour of regional policy were emphasised quite strongly by several respondents, whereas social equity arguments, i.e. the redistributive, resource transfer rationales, were cited less frequently. This would suggest that the locus of the regional policy debate in Ireland is shifting from 'regional equity' to 'regional efficiency'. The need for public services to cohere spatially was also raised.

Current goals

The agenda in terms of defining the overarching goal for regional policy in Ireland has been largely set by the National Spatial Strategy (NSS). Enhancing the potential of each region, rather than reducing disparities, was identified as the current goal by most interviewees, consistent with the alignment of the new NDP with the NSS. Some perceived balanced regional development as a symbolic or populist goal, useful politically but not practically. However, the lack of clear measurable objectives in the NSS renders precise evaluation of the effectiveness of regional policy in Ireland very difficult.

Principal features of regional policy

The interviewees viewed the NSS as the principal instrument of regional policy in Ireland, the intention being that public investment will be aligned with this. Regional policy was perceived as secondary to sectoral policies, and it was acknowledged that sectoral policies can have substantial spatial impacts. Some evidence of a recognition of differential regional needs in enterprise and transport policies was identified, but less so in other sectoral policy domains such as science and innovation.

The absence of structured engagement with regional policy advocates and of a regional political imperative was highlighted, and these were given as reasons for the subsidiary status of regional issues. Funding differentiation was viewed as a weak instrument without policy differentiation. Decentralisation and the redistributive effects of the taxation and welfare systems were also identified as features of regional policy.

Effectiveness of regional policy

The measures of regional performance reviewed in Chapter 4 revealed a mixed picture on the extent and nature of regional disparities in Ireland. Measures of output (GDP/GVA) per capita – the most commonly used indicator of economic performance, notwithstanding the limitations of its applicability in Ireland – indicate continued disparities, while measures of recent regional labour market conditions and disposable incomes reveal some convergence.

All regions have experienced population growth in the past decade, but the largest increases have been in the Dublin commuter belt. Challenges therefore remain in terms of achieving greater balance of economic output levels and productivity, research and innovation performance, and increasing the combined population share of the designated gateways as a counterbalance to the Greater Dublin Area.

Viewed from the perspective of overall national prosperity, regional policy was seen by many interviewees (especially national government interviewees) as having been effective in recent years, but less so when viewed from the perspective of reducing regional disparities. All regions are now much better off, but not equally so. The absence of a generally accepted metric to measure the success of regional policy limits the possibility of objectively assessing its effectiveness.

If the effectiveness of regional policy is contingent on continued economic growth and regional investment, it may prove difficult to avoid widening regional disparities in the context of an economic downturn, in view of the sectoral composition of employment and the relative vulnerabilities of the sectors, which are more prevalent in some regions than in others. Furthermore, the adequacy of the NSS planning framework and process to prevent further unsustainable growth patterns was called into question.

Convergence and divergence forces

Economic disparities as discussed in Chapter 4 have been attributed to productivity differentials, arising from industry structure, demographic factors and the unequal presence of high-value economic activities and multinational companies. Other underlying factors identified were agglomeration effects such as the concentration of innovation and human resource capacity and the stock of public infrastructure, creating an environment more propitious for economic development in cities than in lesser urbanised areas.

Several interviewees predicted that the forces of global economic activity were likely to drive further concentrations of economic activity, and the dominance of the Greater Dublin Area was predicted to continue. Countervailing forces including the potential benefit of investment in regional locations to improve their economic attractiveness and a desire for a better quality of life in non-urbanised locations were identified, but the economic and population imbalances between the Greater Dublin Area and the rest of the country were predicted to remain quite strong. The concentration of high-value activities in a small number of cities is therefore likely to persist in the absence of targeted investment to enhance the productive capacity of all regions in a planned, coherent and integrated manner.

Preferred goals and policy drivers

A majority of interviewees cited competitiveness as their preferred goal, with polycentric spatial structuring and cohesion mentioned less frequently. In the context of the literature on the regional foundations of national competitiveness reviewed in Chapter 2 (Gardiner et al., 2004), interviewees generally viewed regional competitiveness as a contributor to this overall national goal. Cohesion was also supported, on the basis that balanced opportunities and access to services were important. Quality of life and sustainability were also proposed as emerging influential policy drivers by some interviewees. Complementarity between the alternative conceptions of regional policy goals was mentioned frequently, and it was suggested that a focus on the competitiveness of the growth centres in each region, combined with more effective spatial planning, could in time deliver a degree of balanced growth across Ireland.

However, two issues remain: what level of public service provision will there be in underdeveloped areas; and what tolerance will there be for wide disparities in economic activity? The preferred goal as expressed by the interviewees is a measure of regional and national development, but does not capture balance.

Measurement

There was a consensus among the interviewees that regional GDP is not an entirely appropriate measure of regional development. A broad suite of indicators was suggested, many of which have been used in the review of regional socioeconomic trends in Chapter 4. The lack of a single widely accepted measure of the performance of regional policy hinders objective assessments of its success or otherwise. The concept of potential, as defined in the NSS, does not lend itself to measurement.

The regional data monitoring system currently being developed by the Spatial Policy Unit may provide the desired set of regional indicators. In the context of a more competitiveness-driven agenda and a greater appreciation of the regional foundations of national economic wellbeing, as discussed in Chapter 2, measures to capture and benchmark regional competitiveness would appear to be essential.

Investment planning

A large number of interviewees viewed investment planning in Ireland as highly centralised and over-influenced by the sectoral priorities of the main government departments, and as not reflecting the prioritisation put on those projects at regional level. The coherence of this process at regional level was questioned by several interviewees and there was support, in particular among regional interviewees, for a more horizontally integrated process. Most national strategies, e.g. the Strategy for Science, Technology and Innovation, do not have a regional equivalent and no structured regional innovation strategies are in place. The central government view was that spatial integration should take place regionally.

Identified mechanisms to enable spatial integration were spatial proofing of public policy and territorial impact analyses. A further suggestion made was to prepare integrated investment strategies for each region as a complement to the NDP, although it was acknowledged that this would be a complex administrative task. More rigorous appraisal and prioritisation of investment plans was advocated, necessitating an increased capacity and mandate to do this at regional level.

Investment in transport infrastructure and broadband services was identified as a key priority. The prioritisation of transport links to Dublin was noted as having potentially negative impacts on other regions. Enhancement of the performance of indigenous enterprises, especially the level of innovation in order to drive future growth in output and to replace the declining FDI sector, was mentioned frequently. Planned investment in regional public services, particularly health, was raised. The tourism sector was identified as being of strategic importance in underdeveloped regions; the economic development role of higher education institutions was also emphasised.

Spatial planning

The principle of having a coherent spatial planning framework was widely supported, although not all interviewees were confident that the NSS would be successful. Concerns were expressed that there might be too many designated gateways and hubs, thus limiting their potential as drivers of the regional economy and as counterbalances to the Greater Dublin Area. Some interviewees proposed a greater emphasis on economic corridors in order to exploit regional agglomeration effects. However, the value of this approach was questioned by other interviewees.

The NSS was viewed as not having delivered on its objectives, as reflected in increased urban sprawl in recent years. The need for stricter planning enforcement was identified, as well as greater co-ordination of investment at gateway level. It appeared to some that the public sector itself had not shown a strong commitment to the NSS, and that the benefits of more effective spatial planning might be lost as a result.

Territorial governance

It was generally accepted that territorial governance arrangements in Ireland are weak and that some devolution of authority to the regional level is desirable on several grounds. The challenges of implementing this in the centralised and localised Irish administrative and political context were recognised by the interviewees.

Several interviewees identified the absence of a designated unit within government with responsibility for the co-ordination of regional policy as a key weakness. Most of those who expressed an opinion on this issue recommended that an expanded Spatial Policy Unit within the Department of the Environment, Heritage and Local Government should fulfil this role. Some interviewees advocated a new model based on policy co-production. A closer integration of the policies and programmes of government agencies with regional policy objectives was also advocated, along with an enhanced policy analysis capacity within regional bodies. A form of 'regional proofing' of national sectoral policies was proposed.

Role of regional bodies

The regional tier of public administration in Ireland was considered to be functionally limited, financially restricted and under-utilised. While there was some consistency in interviewee viewpoints on the need for a reconfiguration of the existing two tiers of regional administration into a single tier, possibly encompassing other region-level bodies, there was no consistency on the ideal number of regional bodies – a range from four to seven was proposed. A majority of the interviewees suggested that the powers of this tier should be enhanced to fulfil a strategic planning, prioritisation and co-ordination role with the full co-operation of central government and its agencies. However, a radical reconfiguration was perceived as unlikely to gain sufficient political support.

The locus for regional policy determination has largely shifted to the domestic level. In the context of a weakening EU-derived rationale for regional structures, a functional rationale, based on meeting national policy objectives, now exists. The key national policy objectives as they apply to regional policy are now focused on enhancing competitiveness and spatial structuring. An examination of the number, mandate and powers of the regional bodies in order to be coherent with the advancement of these priorities is warranted.

Conclusions and implications for Irish regional policy

Arising from the above findings, conclusions are drawn in this section in relation to the key research questions of the study, and the implications of these conclusions for regional policy in Ireland are then set out.

Regional economic growth patterns

The evident differences in historical resource endowments, market failures and the uneven rates of technological adaptation in Ireland suggest that the market adjustment mechanisms operating through free trade and labour and capital mobility, anticipated by the neoclassical growth model, are unlikely to operate adequately to bring about more balanced regional economic development. Endogenous growth theory provides a strong rationale for public investments that enhance the conditions for economic growth and also for territorial governance systems at national and regional levels that enable effective inter-institutional co-ordination and mobilisation of regional resources.

The persistent divergence in regional productivity levels, analysed in Chapter 4, indicates that the endogenous potential of the regions is unequal and that processes of cumulative causation are at work. This suggests that a regional policy based on exploiting the prospects for productivity growth in each region is the appropriate one. The orientation of public investment around enhancing the growth potential of each of the growth centres, as proposed in the NDP 2007–13, should therefore be pursued. However, the findings of this study demonstrate that the mechanisms by which appropriate investments are identified and prioritised are not working effectively and that the regional governance arrangements required to co-ordinate such an approach are currently too weak to be effective.

Policy drivers: Cohesion, competitiveness and polycentric development

The concept of territorial cohesion embraces the sometimes contradictory goals of economic and social cohesion, competitiveness and spatial structuring, aiming to build on regional strengths while at the same time maintaining the provision of services of general interest. The influence of the EU on triggering institutional and policy reform in the regional policy domain is now significantly reduced in Ireland, and it is likely that pursuit of the goals of the Lisbon competitiveness agenda will be more evident than pursuit of the cohesion agenda, confirming Bachtler and Wishlade's (2004) concerns in relation to the selective application of the loosely defined territorial cohesion agenda. Ireland having been an exponent and beneficiary of economic and social cohesion policies within the EU for two decades, the findings of this study would suggest that Irish regional policy, as fashioned domestically, is now more oriented towards investing where the greatest return can be made rather than towards focusing additional investment in the weaker regions. However, if more balance is to be attained, this approach must be pursued in a manner that enables all regions to enhance their economic potential.

The literature reviewed highlighted a growing recognition of the regional foundations of national competitiveness. This has been given a further impetus by the renewed Lisbon Agenda adopted in 2005, which emphasised the role of regions in advancing competitiveness, innovation performance and employment creation. The primary factors that drive regional competitiveness as described by Walsh (2006) are the level of innovation in organisations, human capital, connectivity infrastructure, economic diversity and strategic capacity at regional level.

This study identified a preference for competitiveness as the primary driver of regional policy, but found that there is limited strategic autonomy at regional level to influence or co-ordinate the factors of regional competitiveness and to develop a 'winning formula' to attract high-growth sectors and a highly skilled workforce, as suggested by Forfás (2004). For instance, there are no regional innovation strategies in place to grow the regional research base and to create the conditions for enhanced interaction and technological diffusion at region level. Further to this, the analysis and benchmarking of competitiveness in Ireland is currently conducted at national level only. This suggests a role for Forfás, in conjunction with strengthened regional bodies, in the benchmarking of regional competitiveness, linked perhaps to the gateway regions.

The pursuit of polycentric urban development whereby proximate dynamic and attractive urban centres develop in a complementary manner requires improved connectivity and institutional co-ordination. The Atlantic Gateways initiative that is now emerging (DEHLG, 2006) gives expression to this concept. The major inter-urban road network currently under construction has prioritised accessibility to Dublin; inter-gateway connectivity along the Atlantic Corridor is a secondary objective.

Tensions are apparent between an approach based on enhancing regional potentials (which are unequal) and the pursuit of spatial equity. The redistributive effects of state transfers have been shown to narrow disparities in disposable incomes, but these do not address the underlying structural deficiencies. Furthermore, labour force migration to regions offering higher quality employment serves to weaken long-term development potential (O'Hara et al., 2008). The optimal approach of 'balanced efficiency' introduced in Chapter 2 would involve the implementation of public investment in a co-ordinated manner that enhances the growth potential and attractiveness of each of the growth centres and its hinterland, recognising the different scales of these urban centres.

The findings of this study suggest that integrated strategies should be prepared for each region to complement the NDP. Territorial governance arrangements need to be strengthened at national and regional levels and spatial planning guidelines at regional level need to be enforced if a degree of balanced efficiency is to be attained.

Investment strategies

The process by which the NDP is prepared would appear to be coherent from the perspective of central government. It draws together the multiannual spending plans of all departments and integrates national strategies into the government's own spending framework. This study found that the sequence in which public investment projects are delivered at regional level by the relevant agencies does not always reflect the prioritisation put on those projects at regional level, and that the spatial impacts of national strategies are not taken adequately into account.

Economic planning in Ireland has traditionally been the almost exclusive preserve of central government, with limited involvement of regional actors. This is sub-optimal and, as Dewhurst (2003) suggests, a national blueprint for regional policy cannot be expected to perform well across all regions of a country; mechanisms to enable regional inputs into the national policy process and into the spatial proofing of national policies are essential. An approach to national and regional planning involving both the NDP and complementary regional strategies, co-produced by national and regional bodies, might be expected to provide a more effective strategic investment framework.

Investment in transport infrastructure was cited in the literature review as a contributor to regional economic efficiency, as it enables a more efficient production environment (Atherton and Johnston, 2005). This study reaffirms the need for an efficient transport network, and a greater priority needs to be given to enhancing the connectivity of the gateways if they are to fulfil their function effectively.

Science and innovation policies have the potential to exacerbate regional disparities if applied in a spatially blind manner. The solution proffered by Perry (2006) – to support selective investments in key regional locations in order to achieve 'balanced excellence' – merits consideration. The regional research base was identified as weak in this study. This supports the case for the elaboration of regional innovation strategies that would encompass research, innovation and technological adaptation strategies and would enhance interactions at regional level. This study also confirmed support for universal broadband availability as a critical enabler of regional economic development.

The potential role of the higher education institutions as loci for knowledge production and technology transfer was highlighted by Thanki (1999), among others. The spatial configuration of Institutes of Technology coincides with the designated gateways and hubs. These institutes can become the loci for knowledge-based enterprise development and the foundations upon which regional research bases, as identified in this study, can be built.

Spatial planning

The spatial structure of a region, long considered a legacy of its past economic development processes, is now recognised to be an important determinant of its future economic development (Parr, 2005a). Spatial planning, 'the contemporary paradigm of regional policy' as defined by Faludi (2006), is an approach focused on achieving the balanced development of strategic urban centres that possess the physical, social and cultural attributes that enable them to be competitive internationally and to drive the economic development of their hinterlands (Fitzpatrick Associates et al., 2006).

This study has found wide acceptance of the NSS as the primary framework for regional policy in Ireland, but there has been little evidence to date of the anticipated prioritisation of investment in the designated growth centres. This is needed in order to create dynamic and attractive urban centres with sufficient connectivity to their hinterlands to generate the critical mass required to increase regional productivity. The proposed Atlantic Gateway initiative has the potential to provide the counterbalance to the Greater Dublin region, one of the objectives of the NSS, but its application to the elongated necklace of gateways along Ireland's western seaboard poses particular challenges in terms of physical and cognitive connectivity and institutional co-ordination. Although there is a planning hierarchy in place linking the NSS through the Regional Planning Guidelines to County and Local Area Plans, the lack of stringent enforcement means that the goals of the NSS are unlikely to be attained.

The continued attraction of FDI to regional centres also provides a strong rationale to pursue this strategy. The NDP Gateway Innovation Fund represents a positive step towards a gateway-centred approach and should be enhanced rather than curtailed as it has now been. The critique of the NSS in Chapter 4, and many of the views expressed in the semi-structured interviews, indicate that the NSS is not being fully delivered, with some suggesting that it needs to be reviewed. However, notwithstanding these criticisms, the broad acceptance of the strategy and the development of a monitoring framework, corridor strategies and stricter enforcement of regional planning regulations indicate that the NSS is providing a platform on which balanced regional efficiency can be pursued.

Territorial governance

Effective territorial governance is required in order to attune policies with a strong territorial focus to differential regional needs and to create the conditions to enable regional competitiveness potential to be enhanced, as suggested by Porter (2003). Following Hutchcroft's (2001) typology of forms of devolution, Ireland's regional devolution arrangement could best be described as 'administrative delegation' involving the transfer of some tasks from central government to other levels. Applying Rhodes's (1996) conception of networked multilevel governance to regional policy suggests that it is the capacity of regional-level institutions to partake actively in inter-organisational networks at multiple levels that is the key determinant of effective regional governance. This implies an enhancement of strategic planning and horizontal co-ordination capacity at regional level and presupposes access to resources and the devolution of some additional authority to that level. This would also make a contribution to democratic engagement and to regional political leadership and consensus-building.

This study found that the territorial dimension of public policy in Ireland is weakly articulated. The 'territorialisation' of national policies necessitates a co-ordinating role at central government level in order to ensure a greater degree of policy differentiation, spatial proofing of sectoral policies and structured mechanisms for interaction with regional interests to identify and address region-specific needs.

Although Regional Development Agencies have been the preferred vehicle to deliver regional economic development strategies in several countries, Irish policy has sought to downgrade rather than enhance their role. A policy co-production approach would require that regional and local tiers acquire the necessary strategic policy analysis capability, resources and authority to enable them to engage more constructively with central government authorities and agencies.

Coherence of Irish regional policy

Policy coherence is synonymous with notions of logical functioning, consistency across policies, co-ordination of policy processes and congruence of policy goals. Following Forster and Stokke's (1999) distinction between internal and external policy consistency, the policy coherence framework developed in this study is applied to regional policy in Ireland. Conclusions are drawn in this section from the findings of this research, applying this policy coherence framework. This is followed by a brief discussion on the use of the policy coherence framework as an analytical framework for public policies.

Internal consistency

Rationale

This study found that there is a strong rationale for regional policy in Ireland based largely on economic efficiency and resource utilisation arguments, while the social equity arguments, i.e. the redistributive rationale and the administrative efficiency justification for regional policy, were cited less frequently. This marks a shift from a traditional redistribution or welfare view of regional policy to an efficiency-based rationale, consistent with the new conception of regions as the arenas for competitive and collaborative advantage and as contributors to overall national wellbeing.

Political leadership

The lack of strong political commitment and leadership on regional policy issues was raised several times by the interviewees. This was attributed to the absence of an electoral imperative at regional level and a lack of engagement with regional policy advocates. The political reality in Ireland is that localised interests predominate, which is not conducive to political buy-in for a more rational evidence-based regional economic and spatial framework, as advocated in this study. Members of regional authorities and assemblies are not directly elected and these bodies do not have fiscal autonomy. The introduction of elections to reformed regional bodies with enhanced responsibilities would introduce an electoral imperative to regional policy in Ireland. At national level, the absence of a government minister with a regional policy brief also limits the opportunity for political leadership on regional policy.

Goals

The goal of regional policy has shifted from one of reducing disparities to enhancing the potential of each region to contribute to overall national development, consistent with the NSS. One consequence of this is that the attainment of this goal does not lend itself to easy measurement. The broad acceptance of one clearly articulated public policy goal and the alignment of the goal of the NSS with the regional objective of the NDP are positive from a policy coherence perspective. Some interviewees viewed the current regional policy goals as symbolic rhetorical objectives.

Institutional arrangements

The institutional arrangements for the design, delivery and co-ordination of regional policy were found to be inadequate at both national and regional levels. There is no designated unit within government with overall responsibility for co-ordinating regional policy and the regional tier was found to be functionally limited, financially restricted and under-utilised. Complementary policies reviewed (transport infrastructure, enterprise, etc.) do have dedicated and effective institutional arrangements in place.

Policy delivery instruments

This study identified a wide range of policy instruments that can be used to further regional policy goals, although regional policy was viewed as subsidiary to sectoral policies. The findings confirm that the rationale for regional policy now derives from enhancing overall economic efficiency and competitiveness. It was also acknowledged that sectoral policies can have substantial spatial impacts. This suggests a need for prioritisation and differentiation of investment to achieve the spatial structuring and enhanced potential of the designated growth centres required to meet this goal. The study found limited evidence of policy differentiation and prioritisation to date, and identified a need for more stringent enforcement of Regional Planning Guidelines.

Resources applied

Regional policy in Ireland operates without a dedicated funding line from central government, although the activities of a wide array of public bodies, each with its own budget, impact substantially on regional areas. Regional policy has to operate within the overall national budgetary framework, as regional bodies do not have fiscal autonomy. The NDP reporting and monitoring framework does not capture detailed expenditure by sub-programme at NUTS II or NUTS III level. It is difficult therefore to discern the level of resources applied to regional policy, as distinct from those that are intended to meet national policy objectives.

Strategic analysis capacity

This study found that there are effective strategic planning, analysis and evaluative capacities at national level, but that these capacities are more limited at regional level. For instance, the assessment and benchmarking of competitiveness is currently an exclusive national competence and is not conducted regionally. In the context of an enhanced role for regional bodies in co-producing integrated regional investment strategies complementary to the NDP, an enhanced capacity to identify, prioritise and evaluate alternative proposals will be required, along with a structured analysis of regional competitiveness.

External coherence

Mutual policy adjustment with the EU

Irish regional policy is now far less influenced by EU programming requirements and the EU support framework is no longer derived from the National Development Plan but from a separate National Strategic

Reference Framework (Government of Ireland, 2007b). The Lisbon Agenda and, to a lesser extent, the principles underlying the European Spatial Development Perspective now have more influence on domestic regional policy than cohesion policy *per se*. This study found that the EU-defined goal of territorial cohesion is not a predominant driver of Irish regional policy.

Subsidiarity

This study found that the principle of subsidiarity was poorly articulated in Irish regional policy. This conforms to the 'functional regionalism' depiction by O'Hara and Commins (2003) or 'administrative delegation' using Hutchcroft's typology (2001), in which regional policies are determined centrally to be administered regionally, but with little or no regional differentiation. The mechanisms for structured engagement with regional bodies will need to be greatly enhanced if the stated goals for regional policy are to be attained.

Structured engagement with non-state actors

The study found very little evidence of structured engagement with non-state actors or regional interest groups. There are ongoing contacts with subnational public bodies and agencies in relation to regional policy issues, and with interest groups in relation to specific projects, but with the exception of the Council for the West there are no organised non-state regional movements with which the state interacts. The general population do not consider themselves as having a stake in regional governance. This, allied to the absence of a regional electoral imperative, contributes to its low prominence in public policy discourse.

Inter-sectoral co-ordination and mutual policy adjustment

The NSS provides the overarching spatial framework for regional policy; other policies are intended to be complementary to this. It is evident from the review of selected policies that the goals of regional policy as set out in the NSS and reinforced in the NDP 2007–13 are more apparent in some strategies (e.g. transport infrastructure) than in others (e.g. science and technology), thus indicating that policy coherence has not been fully attained. The interaction of regional policy with other policy domains to ensure more effective horizontal co-ordination requires a structured form of interaction with regional interests and spatial proofing of sectoral policies, to avoid negative regional outcomes.

Coherence of Irish regional policy: overall conclusion

The overall conclusion that can be drawn from the application of the policy coherence framework is that regional policy in Ireland performs poorly in terms of several, but not all, elements of both internal and external coherence. Although there is a strong rationale for regional policy, the political culture is localised, regional bodies lack an electoral mandate and there is no central department with overall responsibility for regional policy. The goals for regional policy have been aligned with the NSS but are based on enhancing potential, which does not lend itself to measurement. This study found a weak articulation of regional territorial governance and limited policy differentiation. Regional policy operates without a dedicated budget and regional bodies have limited strategic autonomy. This study found limited evidence of subsidiarity and regional policies are largely determined centrally, with few mechanisms for structured engagement with non-state actors. The goals of regional policy were not clearly evident in some of the sectoral policies reviewed.

This conclusion should however be framed in the context of the challenge, discussed in Chapter 2, of attaining absolute policy coherence and mutual policy consistency where there are multiple competing demands, complex multi-tiered governance structures and where political prerogatives may periodically change the scope, objectives or modalities of policy implementation.

Coherence as an analytical framework

The application of the policy coherence framework developed for this study proved to be useful both in defining the themes that were included in the interview guide and in providing a framework within which to focus the conclusions. The use of such a framework in this study illustrates that it could be further developed and applied in the analysis of other policy domains.

A potential limitation of the application of the framework is that it requires structured engagement with a large number of players responsible for the design and delivery of the policy domain, as well as with those responsible for related policy domains (in order to determine mutual policy adjustment) and with other state and non-state actors at different territorial levels, in order to undertake a complete analysis.

Recommendations

Arising from the above conclusions and discussion of policy implications, the following recommendations are made. These are not in any particular order of priority.

Central government co-ordination

A designated unit should be established within government with responsibility for the co-ordination of regional policy, structured engagement with state and non-state regional interests and the introduction of procedures across government to ensure that territorial objectives are better integrated into public policy. An expanded Spatial Policy Unit within the Department of the Environment, Heritage and Local Government may be the most appropriate governmental unit to carry out this function.

Review of regional bodies

A review of the structures, powers and functions of regional bodies in Ireland should be undertaken. A case can be made for a single strengthened regional tier of directly elected regional bodies with the strategic policy analysis and evaluation capability, resources and authority to enable them to engage on an equal footing with central government authorities and agencies and to prepare integrated regional investment strategies as co-equal complements to the NDP investment strategies (see next recommendation).

Integrated regional strategies

A new approach to national and regional investment planning should be introduced for the next multiannual planning framework. This would involve the co-production of national and regional investment strategies by national and regional bodies, consisting of an overarching national development plan and complementary regional investment strategies, with equal status.

Regional innovation strategies

The weak articulation of regional science and innovation policy as found in this study necessitates the development of regional innovation strategies, possibly led by Enterprise Ireland, with the active engagement of all relevant actors. The higher education institutions should become the loci for knowledge-based enterprise development and the foundations on which regional research bases, as identified in this study, can be built, especially in the smaller gateways.

Benchmarking regional competitiveness

As overall national competitiveness cannot be attained without having dynamic competitive regional locations, a far greater focus is now needed on regional competitiveness in public policy. A thorough analysis and benchmarking of competitiveness at an appropriate regional level should be undertaken by the National Competitiveness Council, in conjunction with regional bodies. The outcomes of this process should feed into national and regional investment planning.

Enforcement of regional planning guidelines

There is a need for stronger enforcement of national and regional planning guidelines within the overall planning hierarchy in Ireland. Local authorities should be compelled to demonstrate compliance in respect of County Development Plans and Local Area Plans, and the strategies of individual agencies should also demonstrate compliance.

Measurement and analysis of regional policy outcomes

More detailed analysis of regional economic performance using a suite of indicators, including adjusted regional GVA data to capture the underlying trends, is required. The commitment by the Spatial Policy Unit to produce a suite of regional indicators to feed into the NDP monitoring system and the development of a Gateway Development Index by the regional assemblies are positive steps in this direction. Greater use should be made of statistical measures of dispersion to capture trends in convergence/ divergence over time. A forum of bodies engaged in regional policy analysis should be convened to assess the outcomes of regional analyses, such as those referred to above, and to recommend appropriate policy responses.

Prioritisation of public investment

A more explicit prioritisation of public investment aligned with the NSS and Regional Planning Guidelines frameworks is required. For example, the inter-gateway transport networks, regional ICT infrastructure and applied research capabilities will need to be of a very high quality in the gateways and hubs if these are to fulfil their roles as attractive and dynamic urban centres, providing a real counterbalance to the Greater Dublin Area.

Regional proofing of sectoral strategies

Mechanisms should be put in place to ensure that the regional implications of sectoral policies that have the greatest impact on differential regional development are properly analysed. This could take the form of territorial impact analyses, undertaken under the direction of the unit mentioned under 'Central government co-ordination' above. A greater input into sectoral policy planning by regional bodies would also facilitate this process.

Limitations of this study

It is recognised that the approach adopted to address the research questions had some limitations. This study examined the sectoral strategies in four policy domains only: transport, science and technology, indigenous enterprise and foreign direct investment. These were chosen because of their particular relevance to regional policy and as indicative of other policy domains that are relevant to regional policy. Extending the study to other sectoral domains, in which there are published strategies, might have provided additional examples on which to base the findings in relation to horizontal (inter-sectoral) coherence; however, where other sectoral areas arose in discussions during the interviews, this did not yield a qualitatively different picture of the extent to which regional policy goals are taken into account in the formulation of other sectoral policies.

The selection of interviewees took many criteria into account. It was considered that the 24 interviewees selected represented a wide spectrum of perspectives across the four categories. Other categories could have been added to the study, e.g. EU officials. It was considered that regional policy formulation is now largely determined domestically and that there would be little further added value to be gained from interviewing EU officials. This would have also added cost to the study.

The statistical trend analysis included in Chapter 4 was restricted to six indicator categories only. Consideration was given to extending this to include further indicators such as skills and social deprivation, but it was decided to focus on the main indicators that have been used to track regional socioeconomic progress to date. The inclusion of this analysis was intended to complement the findings of the interviews and to set the analysis of regional disparities and of the national investment and spatial strategies within a statistical context.

Finally, some consideration was given to convening a focus group session in order to discuss the interim findings of the study. This was ruled out both on a practicality/cost basis and on the basis that the purpose of the approach was not to gain consensus on the findings but to elicit the perspectives of each of the interviewees on each of the research themes. A qualitative analysis approach was used to identify the key concepts and to categorise the responses in order to highlight the most significant common responses and those with general applicability.

Areas for further research

The study involved the development and application of a policy coherence framework to assess the regional policy domain in Ireland. This framework could be developed and applied to other policy domains. Further work could be carried out on the development of territorial impact analysis tools that can be used by Irish policymakers. Further analysis could also be conducted of sectoral–spatial trends in Ireland, possibly using econometric models. These could be used to determine the true extent of agglomeration effects as they apply in Ireland.

Concluding comments

The conclusions reached and the recommendations made (above) point towards possible solutions to some of the core dilemmas facing Ireland's regional policy, as touched on in Chapter 2.

1. It may be possible to reconcile cohesion and competitiveness goals within an appropriate spatial and territorial governance framework, to attain an outcome of balanced efficiency.
2. The strengthening forces of agglomeration can be exploited somewhat by enhancing the dynamism of strategically located growth centres that are connected to their hinterlands.
3. The challenges posed in weaker regions in terms of pursuing strategies that have proved effective in more dynamic regions – such as polycentric development, inward investment and regional innovation strategies – necessitate tailored region-specific responses.
4. In the absence of the proofing of sectoral strategies, the differential spatial impacts of R&D, ICT and transport investment strategies may contribute to widening disparities.

Bibliography

Adams J., Robinson P. and Vigor, A. (2003) *A New Regional Policy for the UK*, London: Institute for Public Policy Research

Advisory Expert Committee (1991) *Local Government Reorganisation and Reform* (Barrington Report), Dublin: Government Stationery Office

Afxentiou, P.C. and Serletis, A. (1998) 'Convergence across Canadian Provinces' in *Canadian Journal of Regional Science*, vol. 21, pp. 111–126

Alasai, A. (2003) *Alternative Measures of Territorial Disparity: An Application to Canada*, Paris: OECD

Al-Ubeydli, O. and Kealey, T. (2000) 'Endogenous Growth Theory: A Critique' in *Economic Affairs*, vol. 20, no. 3, pp. 10–13

Angelis, V.A., Gaki, E. and Antivachis, N. (2006) 'Regions, Regional Problems and Regional Policy in the Enlarged EU', paper presented at the Regional Studies Association Conference *Shaping EU Regional Policy: Economic, Social and Political Pressures*, Leuven, Belgium, June; Seaford, UK: Regional Studies Association

Ansell, C. (2000) 'The Networked Polity: Regional Development in Western Europe' in *Governance*, vol. 13, no. 3, pp. 303–333

Armstrong, H. and Taylor, J. (2000) *Regional Economics and Policy* (3rd ed.), Malden, MA: Blackwell

Atherton, A. and Johnston, A. (2005) 'A Taxonomy of Sub-Regional Economies: Identifying "Local Economies" in Regions through Firm Agglomeration and Labour Flow Effects', paper presented to the Regional Science Association (British and Irish Section) Annual Conference, Stratford-upon-Avon, August

Audretsch, D.B. and Keilbach, M. (2004) 'Entrepreneurship Capital and Economic Performance' in *Regional Studies*, vol. 38, no. 8, pp. 949–959

Bachtler, J. and Wishlade, F. (2004) *Search for Consensus: The Debate on Reforming EU Cohesion Policy*, EoRPA Paper 04/4, Glasgow: EPRC

Barro, R.J. and Sala-i-Martin, X. (1995) *Economic Growth*, New York: McGraw-Hill

Barry, F. (2003) 'Economic Integration and Convergence Processes in the EU Cohesion Countries' in *Journal of Common Market Studies*, vol. 41, no. 5, pp. 897–921

BMW Regional Assembly (2008) *Submission to the Green Paper on Local Government*, Ballaghaderreen, www.bmwassembly.ie

Boucher, G. and Collins, G. (2003) 'Having One's Cake and Being Eaten too: Irish Neo-liberal Corporatism' in *Review of Social Economy*, vol. 61, no. 3, pp. 295–316

Boucher, G., Conway, C. and Van der Meer, E. (2003) 'Tiers of Engagement by Universities in Their Region's Development' in *Regional Studies*, vol. 37, no. 9, pp. 887–897

Boyle, G., McCarthy, T. and Walsh, J. (1999) 'Regional Income Differentials and the Issue of Regional Equalisation in Ireland' in *Journal of the Statistical and Social Inquiry Society of Ireland*, vol. 28, part 1, pp. 155–210

Bradley, J. (2002) 'Industrial Strategy and Spatial Planning, North and South: Challenges Facing the Island Economy', Paper presented at *Ireland 2020: People, Place and Space*, National Conference of the Irish Branch of the Regional Studies Association, Bunratty, April

Bradley, J. (2005) 'Has EU Regional Policy Been Effective? The Debate on Structural Funds', paper presented at the 45th Congress of the European Regional Science Association, Amsterdam, August; Dublin: ESRI

Brasili, C. and Gutierrez, L. (2004) *Regional Convergence across the European Union*, Bayreuth, Germany: University of Bayreuth

Bryman, A. (2004) *Social Research Methods* (2nd ed.), London: Oxford University Press

Buchanan, C. and Partners (1968) *Regional Studies in Ireland*, Dublin: An Foras Forbartha

Callinan, B. (2000) *Leaders, Visions and Networks: Ireland's Shannon Story*, Dublin: Irish Academic Press

Cappelen, A., Castellacci, F., Fagerberg, J. and Verspagen, B. (2001) 'The Impact of Regional Support on Growth and Convergence in the European Union', paper presented at the European Meeting on Applied Evolutionary Economics, Vienna, September

Casellas, A. and Galley, C.C. (1999) 'Regional Definitions in the European Union: A Question of Disparities?' in *Regional Studies*, vol. 33, no. 6, pp. 551–558

Central Statistics Office (2005) *Regional Population Projections 2006–2021*, Dublin: CSO

Central Statistics Office (2006) *Census 2006: Preliminary Results*, Dublin: CSO

Central Statistics Office (2007) *Quarterly National Household Survey*, Dublin: CSO

Central Statistics Office (2008) *County Incomes and Regional GDP 2005*, Dublin: CSO

CIRCA (2004) *Audit of Innovation in the BMW Region: Final Report*, BMW Regional Assembly, www.bmwassembly.ie

Collins, P. (2002) *Policy Approaches to Developing the Region in the Information Age: Differentiating Information Economy from Information Society at the Regional Level*, Galway: Centre for Innovation and Structural Change

Commins, P. (2006) 'Economic Development Issues in Sparsely Populated Regions: Illustrations from Ireland's BMW Region', Paper presented at the EKIE Conference, Galway, March

Commission of the European Communities (1999) *European Spatial Development Perspective: Towards Balanced and Sustainable Development of the Territory of the European Union*, Brussels: European Commission

Commission of the European Communities (2004a) *A New Partnership for Cohesion, Convergence, Competitiveness, Co-operation: Third Report on Economic and Social Cohesion*, Luxembourg: Office for Official Publications of the European Communities

Commission of the European Communities (2004b) *Innovate for a Competitive Europe: A New Action Plan for Innovation*, Brussels: European Commission

Commission of the European Communities (2006a) *Community Strategic Guidelines on Cohesion 2007–13*, Brussels: European Commission

Commission of the European Communities (2006b) *The Growth and Jobs Strategy and the Reform of European Cohesion: Fourth Progress Report on Cohesion*, Brussels: European Commission

Commission of the European Communities (2006c) *Innovative Strategies and Actions: Results from 15 Years of Regional Experimentation*, European Commission Working Document, Brussels: European Commission

Commission of the European Communities (2006d) *Bridging the Broadband Gap: Communication from the Commission to the Council, the European Parliament, the European Economic and Social Committee and the Committee of the Regions*, Brussels: European Commission

Commission of the European Communities (2008) *Green Paper on Territorial Cohesion: Turning Diversity into Strength*, Brussels: European Commission

Crang, M. (2002) 'Qualitative Methods: The New Orthodoxy?' in *Progress in Human Geography*, vol. 26, no. 5, pp. 647–655

Crossman, F. (2003) 'Research Philosophy: Towards an Understanding' in *Nurse Researcher*, vol. 11, no. 1, pp. 46–55

Crotty, M. (2003) *The Foundations of Social Research: Meaning and Perspective in the Research Process*, London: Sage

Dall'erba, S. and Le Gallo, J. (2003) 'Regional Convergence and the Impact of European Structural Funds over 1989–1999: A Spatial Econometric Analysis', paper presented at European Union Studies Association Biennial Conference, Nashville, TN, March

Danson, M. (2003) 'Regional Economic Development, Agencies and Competitiveness: A European Perspective' in E. O'Leary (ed.) *Irish Regional Development: A New Agenda*, Dublin: Liffey Press

Department of Enterprise, Trade and Employment (2004) *Enterprise Strategy Group Action Plan*, www.entemp.ie

Department of Enterprise, Trade and Employment (2005) 'Minister Martin announces new mandate for Shannon Development' (press release), www.entemp.ie

Department of Enterprise, Trade and Employment (2006) *Strategy for Science, Technology and Innovation 2006–13*, Dublin: Government Stationery Office

Department of the Environment, Heritage and Local Government (2002) *National Spatial Strategy 2002–2020: People, Places and Potential*, Dublin: Government Stationery Office

Department of the Environment, Heritage and Local Government (2006) *Atlantic Gateways Initiative: Achieving Critical Mass*, Dublin: Government Stationery Office

Department of the Environment, Heritage and Local Government (2008) *Green Paper on Local Government Reform and Stronger Local Democracy: Options for Change*, Dublin: Government Stationery Office

Department of Transport (2008) *Transport 21: Second Annual Progress Report to the Government 2007*, Dublin: Government Stationery Office

Dewhurst, J. (2003) 'Industry Performance and Regional Growth: Lessons for Irish Policymakers' in E. O'Leary (ed.) *Irish Regional Development: A New Agenda*, Dublin: Liffey Press

Di Francesco, M. (2001) 'Process not Outcomes in New Public Management? Policy Coherence in Australian Government' in *The Drawing Board*, vol. 1, no. 3, pp. 103–116

Enterprise Ireland (2007) *Transforming Irish Industry 2008–2010*, www.enterprise-ireland.com

Enterprise Strategy Group (2004) *Ahead of the Curve*, Dublin: Forfás

European Spatial Planning Observatory Network (2004) *Potentials for Polycentric Development in Europe*, www.espon.eu

European Spatial Planning Observatory Network (2006) *ESPON Atlas: Mapping the Structure of the European Territory*, www.espon.eu

European Union (2006) *EU Mechanisms that Promote Policy Coherence for Development: A Scoping Study*, Maastricht, The Netherlands: European Union Evaluation Studies

Expert Group on Future Skills Needs (2006) *Skills at Regional Level in Ireland: A Study of Skills Demand at Regional Level for Specified Enterprise Sectors*, Dublin: Forfás

Fáilte Ireland (2008) *Tourism Facts 2007*, Dublin: Fáilte Ireland

Faludi, A. (2006) 'From European Spatial Development to Territorial Cohesion Policy' in *Regional Studies*, vol. 40, no. 6, pp. 667–678

Fay, B. (1996) *Contemporary Philosophy of Social Science*, Malden, MA: Blackwell

Felsenstein, D. and Portnov, B.A. (2005) 'Understanding Regional Inequalities in Small Countries' in *Regional Studies*, vol. 39, no. 5, pp. 647–658

Fitzgerald, J., Kearney, I., Morgenroth, E. and Smyth, D. (1999) *National Investment Priorities for the Period 2000–2006*, Policy Research Series No. 33, Dublin: Economic and Social Research Institute, www.esri.ie

Fitzgerald, J., McCarthy, C., Morgenroth, E. and O'Connell, P. (2003) *The Mid-Term Evaluation of the National Development Plan and Community Support Framework for Ireland 2000 to 2006*, Dublin: Economic and Social Research Institute, www.esri.ie

Fitzgerald, J. and Morgenroth, E. (2006) *Ex Ante Evaluation of the Investment Priorities for the National Development Plan 2007–2013*, Dublin: Economic and Social Research Institute, www.esri.ie

International Centre for Local and Regional Development, Brady Shipman Martin and Fitzpatrick Associates (2006) *Implementing the NSS: Gateway Investment Priorities Study*, Dublin: Forfás

Forfás (2004) *Annual Competitiveness Report, 2004*, Dublin: Forfás

Forfás (2005) *International Trade and Investment Report 2004: A Report by Forfás to the Trade Advisory Forum and the Foreign Earnings Committee*, Dublin: Forfás

Forfás (2006a) *Annual Competitiveness Report 2006, Volume 1: Benchmarking Ireland's Performance*, Dublin: Forfás

Forfás (2006b) *Innovation Survey 2006*, Dublin: Forfás

Forster, J. and Stokke, O. (eds) (1999) *Policy Coherence in Development Cooperation*, London: Frank Cass

Fresco, L.O. (2004) 'Policy Coherence for Agriculture and Development' in *FAO Spotlight*, June, Rome: Food and Agriculture Organisation

Fujita, M. (1988) 'A Monopolistic Competition Model of Spatial Agglomeration: A Differentiated Product Approach' in *Regional Science and Urban Economics*, vol. 18, pp. 87–124

Gardiner B., Martin R. and Tyler, P. (2004) 'Competitiveness, Productivity and Economic Growth across the European Regions' in *Regional Studies*, vol. 38, no. 9, pp. 1045–1067

Giannias, D., Liargovis, P. and Manola, G. (1999) 'Quality of Life Indices for Analysing Convergence in the European Union' in *Regional Studies*, vol. 33, no. 1, pp. 27–35

Glaser, B.G. and Strauss, A.L. (1967) *The Discovery of Grounded Theory: Strategies for Quantitative Research*, Chicago: Aldine

Glen, C. (2000) *Regional Convergence and Regional Policy in the European Union*, Valdosta, GA: Valdosta State University

Governa, F. and Santangelo, M. (2006) 'Territorial Governance and Territorial Cohesion in the European Scenario', paper presented at the Regional Studies Association Conference *Shaping EU Regional Policy: Economic Social and Political Pressures*, Leuven, Belgium, June; Seaford, UK: Regional Studies Association

Government of Ireland (1999) *National Development Plan 2000–2006*, Dublin: Government Stationery Office

Government of Ireland (2006) *Towards 2016: Ten-Year Framework Social Partnership Agreement*, Dublin: Government Stationery Office

Government of Ireland (2007a) *National Development Plan 2007–13, Transforming Ireland: A Better Quality of Life for All*, Dublin: Government Stationery Office

Government of Ireland (2007b) *National Strategic Reference Framework: Supporting and Enabling Dynamic Regions*, Dublin: Government Stationery Office

Graham, B. and Hart, M. (1999) 'Cohesion and Diversity in the European Union: Irreconcilable Forces' in *Regional Studies*, vol. 33, no. 3, pp. 259–268

Hayward, K. (2006) 'A Marriage of Convenience: The EU and Regionalization in Ireland', paper delivered to the Political Science Association of Ireland Annual Conference, Cork, October

Heraud, J.A. and Koschatzky, K. (2006) 'Regions, Universities and Excellence in Europe' in *Regions*, no. 263, Autumn

Herz, B. (2002) *Real Convergence and Regional Policy in the European Union: Evidence from the 1990s*, Working Paper, Bayreuth University, Bayreuth, Germany

Hill, M. (1997) *The Policy Process in the Modern State* (3rd ed.), London: Prentice Hall

Hill, M. and Hupe, P. (2002) *Implementing Public Policy*, London: Sage

Hofer, H. and Wörgöter, A. (1997) 'Regional per capita income convergence in Austria' in *Regional Studies*, vol. 31, no. 1, pp. 1–12

Hooghe, L. and Marks, G. (2001) *Multi-level Governance and European Integration*, Oxford: Rowman and Littlefield

Hutchcroft, P.D. (2001) 'Centralisation and Decentralisation in Administration and Politics: Assessing Territorial Dimensions of Authority and Power' in *Governance*, vol. 14, no. 1, pp. 24–53

Industrial Development Authority Ireland (2008) *IDA Ireland End of Year Statement 2007*, Dublin: IDA

Irish Business and Employers Confederation (2006) *National Development Plan: A New Approach to Balanced Regional Development*, Dublin: IBEC

Jones, M., Goodwin, M. and Jones, R. (2005) 'State Modernization, Devolution and Economic Governance: An Introduction and Guide to Debate' in *Regional Studies*, vol. 39, no. 4, pp. 397–403

Jordan, D. and O'Leary, E. (2005) 'The Roles of Interaction and Proximity for Innovation by Irish High-Technology Businesses: Policy Implications' in *Quarterly Economic Commentary, Summer 2005*, Dublin: Economic and Social Research Institute

Keane, M. and Garvey, E. (2006) 'Measuring the Employment Effects of the Rural Renewal Tax Scheme' in *Regional Studies*, vol. 40, no. 3, pp. 359–374

Keating, M. (1997) 'The Political Economy of Regionalism' in M. Keating and J. Loughlin (eds) *The Political Economy of Regionalism*, London: Frank Cass

Keating, M. (2000) *The New Regionalism in Western Europe: Territorial Restructuring and Political Change*, Cheltenham, UK: Edward Elgar

Krugman, P. (1991) 'Increasing Returns and Economic Geography' in *Journal of Political Economy*, vol. 99, no. 3, pp. 483–499

Kuhn, T.S. (1970) *The Structure of Scientific Revolutions* (2nd ed.), Chicago: University of Chicago Press

Kvale, S. (1996) *Interviews: An Introduction to Qualitative Research Interviewing*, Thousand Oaks, CA: Sage

Laffan, B. (1996) 'Ireland: A Region without Regions – The Odd Man Out' in L. Hooghe (ed.), *Cohesion Policy and European Integration*, London: Oxford University Press

Laffan, B. (2004) *Multilevel Governance: The Dynamics of EU Cohesion Policy – A Comparative Analysis*, Dublin: Dublin European Institute

Leech, B.L. (2002) 'Asking Questions: Techniques for Semi-structured Interviews' in *Political Science and Politics*, vol. 35, no. 4, pp. 665–668

Lincoln, Y.S. and E. Guba (1985) *Naturalistic Inquiry*, Thousand Oaks, CA: Sage

Lipshitz, G. (1995) 'Regional Disparities: The Canadian Case in the Theoretical Context' in *Canadian Journal of Regional Science*, vol. 18, no. 3, pp. 357–378

López-Bazo, E. and Moreno, R. (2007) 'Regional heterogeneity in the private and social returns to human capital' in *Spatial Economic Analysis*, vol. 2, no. 1, pp. 23–44

MacSharry, R. and White, P. (2000) *The Making of the Celtic Tiger: The Inside Story of Ireland's Boom Economy*, Dublin: Mercier Press

Maillet, D. (1997) 'Innovative milieux and new generations of regional policies' in D. McCafferty and J. Walsh (eds) *Competitiveness, Innovation and Regional Development in Ireland*, Dublin: Regional Studies Association

Martin, P. (2000) 'The Role of Public Policy in the Process of Regional Convergence', paper prepared for the Conference on Regional Development Policy and Convergence in the EU, Brussels: European Investment Bank Papers

Martin, R.L. (2003) *A Study on the Factors of Regional Competitiveness: A Final Report for the European Commission Directorate-General Regional Policy*, Cambridge: Cambridge Econometrics

McAleer, J. (2007) 'Regional Governance in Ireland – Reflections from a Practitioner at the Coalface', paper presented at the Southern and Eastern Regional Assembly Annual Conference, April

McGowan, L. and Murphy, M. (2003) 'Europeanisation and the Irish Experience' in M. Adshead and M. Millar (eds) *Public Administration and Public Policy in Ireland*, London: Routledge

Morgan, G. and Smircich, L. (1980) 'The Case for Qualitative Research' in *Academy of Management Review*, vol. 5, no. 4, pp. 491–500

Morgan, K. (2002) 'The English Question: Regional Perspectives on a Fractured Nation' in *Regional Studies*, vol. 37, no. 7, pp. 797–810

Morgenroth, E. (2000) 'Regionalisation and the Functions of Regional and Local Government' in A. Barrett (ed.) *Budget Perspectives*, Dublin: Economic and Social Research Institute, www.esri.ie

Morgenroth, E. (2003a) *An Assessment of the National Spatial Strategy*, Dublin: Economic and Social Research Institute, www.esri.ie

Morgenroth, E. (2003b) 'What Should Irish Policymakers Learn from Recent Advances in Growth Theory and Economic Geography?' in E. O'Leary (ed.) *Irish Regional Development: A New Agenda*, Dublin: Liffey Press

Morgenroth, E. (2006) *Economic Integration and Structural Change: The Case of Irish Regions*, Dublin: Economic and Social Research Institute, www.esri.ie

Morgenroth, E. (2007a) 'Trends in the Regional Economic Activity of Ireland: The Role of Productivity' in *Perspectives on Irish Productivity: A Selection of Essays by Irish and International Economists*, Dublin: Forfás

Morgenroth, E. (2007b) 'The Regional Dimension of Taxes and Public Expenditure in Ireland', ESRI Working Paper no. 195, Dublin: Economic and Social Research Institute, www.esri.ie

Morgenroth, E. and Fitzgerald, J. (2006) *Ex Ante Evaluation of the Investment Priorities for the National Development Plan 2007–13*, Policy Research Series no. 59, Dublin: Economic and Social Research Institute, www.esri.ie

Myrdal, G. (1957) *Economic Theory and Underdeveloped Regions*, London: Duckworth Press

National Economic and Social Council (1997) *Population Distribution and Economic Development: Trends and Policy Implications*, Report no. 102, Dublin: NESC

National Economic and Social Council (2005) *NESC Strategy 2006: People, Productivity and Purpose*, Dublin: NESC

National Economic and Social Council (2008) *The Irish Economy in the 21st Century*, Report no. 117, Dublin: NESC

O'Hara, P., (2002) 'Social Partnership and Regional Development' in S. Healy and B. Reynolds (eds) *Choosing a Fairer Future: An Agenda for Social Partnership after the Celtic Tiger*, Dublin: CORI Justice Commission

O'Hara, P. and Commins, P. (2003) 'Ireland and the Future of Europe: A Regional Perspective' in S. Healy and B. Reynolds (eds) *Ireland and the Future of Europe: Leading the Way towards Inclusion?*, Dublin: CORI Justice Commission

O'Hara, P., Frost, D., McHenry, H. and White, P. (2008) 'The Regional Development Challenge: A Western Region Perspective', paper delivered to *Delivering Balanced Regional Development* Conference, Athlone, May; Ballaghaderreen: Western Development Commission, www.wdc.ie

O'Leary, E. (1999) 'Regional Income Estimates for Ireland, 1995' in *Regional Studies*, vol. 33, no. 9, pp. 805–814

O'Leary, E. (2002) 'Sources of Regional Divergence in the Celtic Tiger: Policy Responses', paper presented to the Statistical and Social Inquiry Society of Ireland, November

O'Leary, E. (2003) 'A Critical Evaluation of Irish Regional Policy' in E. O'Leary (ed.) *Irish Regional Development: A New Agenda*, Dublin: Liffey Press

O'Leary, E. (2007) 'Regional Policy and Agglomeration Economies in Ireland' in *Perspectives on Irish Productivity: A Selection of Essays by Irish and International Economists*, Dublin: Forfás

Organisation for Economic Co-operation and Development (1996) *Building Policy Coherence: Tools and Tensions*, Paris: OECD Publishing

Organisation for Economic Co-operation and Development (2005) *OECD Regions at a Glance*, Paris: OECD Publishing

Organisation for Economic Co-operation and Development (2006) *Higher Education in Ireland*, Paris: OECD Publishing

Paci, R. and Pigliaru, F. (1999) *Technological Catch-up and Regional Convergence in Europe*, CRENOS Working Paper 99/9, Cagliari, Italy: University of Cagliari

Parr, J. B. (2001) 'Regional Economic Planning: Learning from Past Experience' in D. Felsenstein et al. (eds) *Public Investment and Regional Economic Development*, Cheltenham, UK: Edward Elgar

Parr, J. B. (2004) 'The Polycentric Urban Region: A Closer Inspection' in *Regional Studies*, vol. 38, no. 3, pp. 231–240

Parr, J. B. (2005a) 'Spatial Planning: Too Little or Too Much' in *Scienze Regionali*, vol. 4, no. 2, pp. 113–129

Parr, J. B. (2005b) 'Perspectives on the City-Region' in *Regional Studies*, vol. 39, no. 5, pp. 555–566

Perry, B. (2006) 'Global Excellence, Local Funding' in *Regions*, no. 263, Autumn

Pike, A., Rodríguez-Pose A. and Tomaney, J. (2006) *Local and Regional Development*, London: Routledge

Porter, M. (2003) 'The Economic Performance of Regions' in *Regional Studies*, vol. 37, no. 6, pp. 549–578

Pritchett, L. (1996) *Population Growth, Factor Accumulation and Productivity*, Policy Research Department Working Paper 1567, New York: World Bank

Quah, D. (1996) 'Twin Peaks: Growth and Convergence in Models of Distribution Dynamics' in *Economics Journal*, vol. 106, pp. 1045–1055

Rhodes, R.A.W. (1994) 'The Hollowing Out of the State: The Changing Nature of the Public Service in Britain' in *Political Quarterly*, vol. 65, no. 2, pp. 138–151

Rhodes, R.A.W. (1996) 'The New Governance: Governing without Government' in *Political Studies*, vol. 44, pp. 652–667

Rodrígues-Pose, A. and Gill, N. (2005) 'On the Economic Dividend of Devolution' in *Regional Studies*, vol. 39, no. 4, pp. 405–420

Romer, P.M. (1986) 'Increasing Returns and Long Run Growth' in *Journal of Political Economy*, vol. 94, pp. 1002–1037

Rosik, P. (2006) 'Transport Infrastructure, Public Capital and Regional Policy – Review of Studies', paper presented at the Regional Studies Association Conference *Shaping EU Regional Policy: Economic Social and Political Pressures*, Leuven, Belgium, June; Seaford, UK: Regional Studies Association

Sala-i-Martin, X. (1994) *Regional Cohesion: Evidence and Theories of Regional Growth and Convergence*, Discussion Paper 1075, London: Centre for Economic Policy Research

Santinha, G., Castro, E. and Subrol, N. (2006) 'Regional Policy Making in the Information and Knowledge Society: ICT Spatial Impacts and Its Importance to Spatial Planning', paper presented at the Regional Studies Association Conference *Shaping EU Regional Policy: Economic Social and Political Pressures*, Leuven, Belgium, June; Seaford, UK: Regional Studies Association

Sarantakos, S. (2005) *Social Research* (3rd ed.), Basingstoke, UK: Palgrave Macmillan

Solow, R. (1956) 'A contribution to the theory of economic growth' in *Quarterly Journal of Economics*, vol. 70, pp. 65–94

Steyvers, K. (2002) 'Regionalisation as a motor for innovation in Flanders: a mantra of political renewal', Paper presented at the 8th Annual European Summer School in Local Government Studies, Cork, July

Thanki, R. (1999) 'How Do We Know the Value of Higher Education to Regional Development?' in *Regional Studies*, vol. 33, no. 1, pp. 84–89

Van der Kamp, H.W. (2006) 'Population Growth: A Doubling of Ireland's Population Possible?', President's address to the Irish Planning Institute National Planning Conference 2006, Dublin: Irish Planning Institute

Venables, A.J. (1996) 'Equilibrium locations of vertically linked industries' in *International Economic Review*, vol. 37, pp. 341–359

Walsh, J. (2005) 'Spatial Development of Europe's North Western Periphery', paper presented to European Spatial Observatory Network, Queen's University Belfast, February

Walsh, B. (2006) 'Labour Market Adjustments in the Irish Regions, 1988–2005' in *Economic and Social Research Institute Quarterly Economic Commentary*, October, Dublin: ESRI, www.esri.ie

Ward, N. (2008) 'Balanced Regional Development: Issues and Insights', paper delivered to Delivering Balanced Regional Development Conference, Athlone, May; Ballaghaderreen: Western Development Commission, www.wdc.ie

Weith, T. and Zillmer, S. (2006) 'Regions in between – no perspective for peripheral areas', paper presented at the Regional Studies Association Conference *Shaping EU Regional Policy: Economic Social and Political Pressures*, Leuven, Belgium, June; Seaford, UK: Regional Studies Association

Welch, C., Marschan-Piekkari, R., Penttinen, H. and Tahvanainen, M. (1999) 'Interviewing Elites in International Organisations: A Balancing Act for the Researcher', paper presented at the 25th Annual Conference of EIBA, Manchester, December

Williamson, J.G. (1965) 'Regional Inequalities and the Process of National Development' in *Economic Development and Structural Change*, vol. 13, pp. 1–84

Glossary

BMW	Border, Midlands and Western Region
CEC	Commission of the European Community
CSO	Central Statistics Office
DEHLG	Department of the Environment, Heritage and Local Government
EGFSN	Expert Group on Future Skills Needs
EI	Enterprise Ireland
ERDF	European Regional Development Fund
ESDP	European Spatial Development Perspective
ESF	European Social Fund
ESPON	European Spatial Observatory Network
ESRI	Economic and Social Research Institute
EU	European Union
FDI	foreign direct investment
GDA	Greater Dublin Area
GDP	gross domestic product
GNP	gross national product
GVA	gross value added
HEI	higher education institution
HPSU	high potential start-up
IBEC	Irish Business and Employers Confederation
ICT	information and communication technologies
IDA	Industrial Development Authority
IoT	Institute of Technology
LEADER	Liaisons Entre Actions de Développement de l'Economie Rurale
NDP	National Development Plan
NESC	National Economic and Social Council
NSRF	National Strategic Reference Framework
NSS	National Spatial Strategy
NUTS	Nomenclature Units for Territorial Statistics
OECD	Organisation for Economic Co-operation and Development
OP	Operational Programme
PRTLI	Programme for Research in Third Level Institutions

QNHS	Quarterly National Household Survey
R&D	research and development
RDA	Regional Development Agency
S&E	Southern and Eastern Region
SFI	Science Foundation Ireland
SMEs	small and medium-sized enterprises
SPU	Spatial Policy Unit
SSTI	Strategy for Science, Technology and Innovation
SWOT	strengths, weaknesses, opportunities and threats
WDC	Western Development Commission

Appendix 1: List of Interviewees

Academic
Edgar Morgenroth, Regional Economist, ESRI
Eoin O'Leary, Regional Economist, University College Cork
Jim Walsh, Geographer and Vice President, NUI Maynooth
Brigid Laffan, College of Human Sciences, University College Dublin
Bridget Quinn, Department of Politics, University of Limerick
Jim Fitzpatrick, Economist and Programme Evaluator

Regional bodies
Brian Callinan, Planning Officer, Shannon Development
Padraig Ó hAoláin, CEO, Údarás na Gaeltachta
Patricia O'Hara, Director of Policy, Western Development Commission
Jim McGovern, Director, West Regional Authority
John McAleer, Director, South-West Regional Authority
Gerry Finn, Director, BMW Regional Assembly
Pat Gallagher, Manager, Offaly County Council (Local Authority)

Social partners[241]
Ray Farrelly, Irish Business and Employers Confederation
Seamus Boland, CEO, Irish Rural Link
Peter Sweeney, Chief Economist, Irish Congress of Trade Unions
Rory O'Donnell, Director, National Economic and Social Council

National bodies
Demot Nolan, Principal Officer, NDP, Department of Finance
David Walsh, Principal Officer, Department of the Environment, Heritage and Local Government
Declan Hughes, Divisional Manager, Competitiveness, Forfás
Brendan Flood, Head of Entrepreneurship and Regions, Enterprise Ireland
John O'Brien, Head of Regions, IDA Ireland

241 The National Economic and Social Council is not strictly a social partner. It reports to the Taoiseach (Prime Minister) on strategic economic and social issues and on the negotiation of agreements with the social partners.

Maurice Treacy, Principal Officer, Transport Policy, Department of Transport
Aidan Hodson, Principal Officer, Office of Science and Technology, Department of Enterprise, Trade and Employment

Appendix 2:
Interview Guide

Question 1: Rationale
Do you think that Ireland should have a regional policy and what should the main elements of that policy be?

Question 2: Goal of current regional policy
What do you consider to be the principal features of Irish regional policy and what would you consider its goals to be?

Question 3: Evaluate regional policy
How effective do you believe current regional policy is?

Question 4: Convergence/divergence forces
What forces do you consider are driving regional convergence and/or divergence in Ireland?

Question 5: Overarching goal/driver
Which of these would you consider should be the predominant goal of Irish regional policy?

- Cohesion – convergence in the economic performance of all regions
- Competitiveness – raising productivity and employment levels, nationally and/or regionally
- Polycentric development – more balanced spatial structuring

Question 6: Measurement criteria
By what criteria should comparative regional performance be measured and evaluated?

Question 7: Investment planning
What types of investment policies would you consider most conducive to achieving your suggested goal for regional policy?

Question 8: Spatial planning
How would you suggest that more effective spatial planning could be achieved in Ireland?

Question 9: Governance arrangements
Who do you consider should be responsible for drawing up, implementing and evaluating investment plans and spatial frameworks?

Question 10: Implications for regional bodies
What specific roles should be played by region-level bodies and what powers (if any) should be devolved to regional bodies?

Appendix 3: Letter to Interviewees

Dear

Over the past three years I have been undertaking a part-time Doctorate in Governance provided by the Institute of Public Administration, Dublin and the Institute of Governance, Queen's University Belfast. This is a four year part-taught, part-thesis programme and I am supported by the Border, Midland and Western Regional Assembly (my employer) and the Local Government Management Services Board.

For my doctoral thesis I propose to examine the coherence of regional policy in Ireland. This will comprise a review of relevant literature, socioeconomic trends and recent policy approaches, and I also intend to interview c. 25 'elite' respondents from academia, government departments and agencies, regional bodies and social partner organisations, using a semi-structured format in order to elicit their views on:

- the rationale, goals, effectiveness and coherence of Irish regional policy;
- cohesion, competitiveness and polycentric development as alternative overarching policy goals/drivers; and
- implications of preferred policy goals for investment strategies, spatial planning and regional governance arrangements in Ireland.

It is proposed to conduct the interviews over the next 2–3 months at times and places convenient to interviewees. I attach a copy of the interview guide, around which the semi-structured interviews will be broadly based. It is my intention to record the interviews and to write up complete transcripts (for validation purposes). In accordance with social research ethical guidelines, respondents are assured of absolute confidentiality and statements will not be attributed to individuals without their express consent. My Thesis Supervisor is Professor Frank Gaffikin, School of Planning, Queen's University Belfast (F.Gaffikin@qub.ac.uk).

I would be grateful if you would consent to be an interviewee for this research. I will contact you shortly in relation to this. If you would like to contact me directly, my mobile number is 087 2253422 or email kmoylan@bmwassembly.ie

Yours sincerely,

Kieran Moylan

Index